AF505033

MUSIC

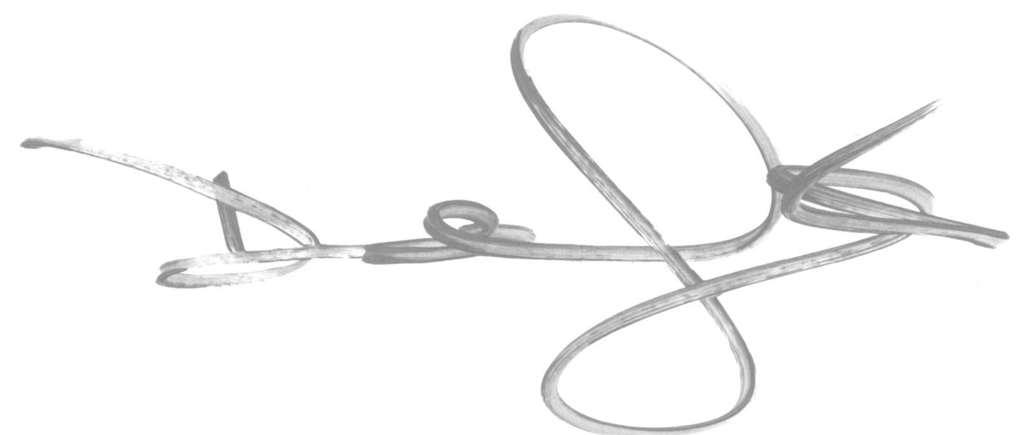

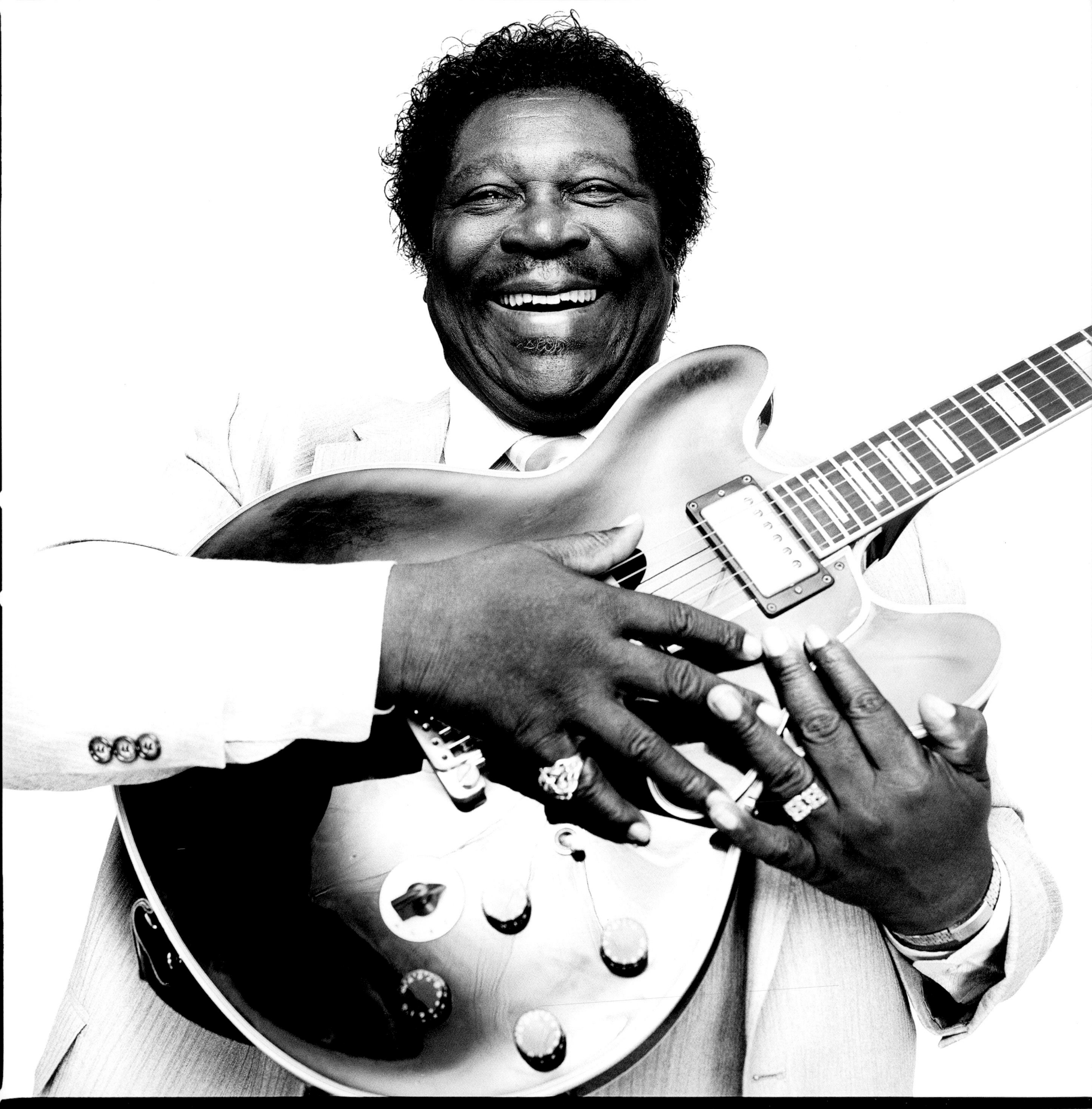

MUSIC

PHOTOGRAPHS BY DEBORAH FEINGOLD

INTRODUCTION BY ANTHONY DeCURTIS

DAMIANI

BY ANTHONY DeCURTIS

Ayouthful Peter Gabriel, his hands flat and his fingers outstretched, his eyes cast upward with hope, striking the pose of a mime, crawling up the inside of a window, trapped as if within a prison—or within his own creativity.

Bono, with an impossible hairdo and an even more impossible belt, looking into the camera as if it were a mirror, characteristically unable to decide if he is on stage or in the privacy of his bedroom (a false distinction?) checking out his look.

L.L. Cool J, chilling (with the help of a hand-held fan) in his room in his grandmother's basement in Queens, at ease amid the avalanche of his things, all the possessions and obsessions that fuel the roughness, whimsy, and winningness of his rhymes.

Prince on the couch in his dressing room in a kind of parody of relaxation, staring straight at the camera, his legs spread, his shirt open, seduction, vulnerability, fear, and threat all intermingling, jostling for prominence, within the complex cocktail mix of his personality.

The Replacements, too, perch on a battered couch as if in their parents' rec room—their fuck-you (or really fuck-us) ease belying the danger of those railroad tracks the couch straddles. With casually self-destructive nonchalance, they're ready for whatever comes—or, at least, they think they are.

Those images, whether in stark black and white or, in L.L.'s case, bursting with color, all reflect their subjects in telling ways. Indeed, it's as if they were expressions of the subjects themselves rather than the creation of another person. Such is the empathetic art of Deborah Feingold, a photographer who for more than three decades has revealed striking truths about the people she views through her lens. This book concentrates on her work with musicians. The images are a kind of secret collaboration, sometimes even an unwilling one, an unspoken agreement that, in exchange for their making themselves available to her eye, Feingold will render a character study that speaks with warmth and gracefulness about both the artist and the art.

That so many of these pictures were taken on the fly, products of the seemingly never-ending battle between record company scheduling demands, musicians' primitive reluctance to have their souls captured in the magic box of the camera, and artists' genuine aesthetic need to communicate meaningfully with an audience who loves or might come to love their music, speaks to the pragmatic generosity of Feingold's gift. These photos are not the result of clever concepts into which a subject has been inserted almost as a kind of afterthought, as if they were mere characters cast in someone else's play. Their fascination and intrigue emerge from the hum and buzz of musicians' everyday lives, just as an idea for a tune might occur to a songwriter from a snippet of conversation overheard on the street or the la-la-la melody of a nursery rhyme a child recites. Musicians express their musicality at all times, these images suggest. And like a skilled producer in a studio, a deft photographer can both encourage that music to come forth, recognize it when it does, and capture it for posterity.

Feingold's vision began to take shape after she graduated from Emerson College in Boston and took a part-time job in a camera store that was located near Paul's Mall and the Jazz Workshop, two essential hotspots of that city's hip cultural life in the sixties and seventies. Those venues became sources of Feingold's musical education—that is, beyond the pop radio nirvana of the fifties and sixties that lit up her youth—and the beginning of her understanding of what spellbinding subjects musicians can be. There and at the Sugar Shack, an R&B hotbed in Boston, she saw the likes of Miles Davis, Bill Withers, and Ashford & Simpson perform. She joined a photo co-op in Cambridge and simultaneously fell in with a group of young jazz musicians. It was a heady time. "It was the early seventies," she says. "It was very free-form, and I'd never been happier. Being around jazz musicians, I learned how to improvise. That changed my life. It was risk-taking and it was exciting."

When her boyfriend, a jazz musician, decided he wanted to move to New York, Feingold decided that might be the right move for her as well. They settled in Chelsea, something of an edgy neighborhood at the time, and when her boyfriend joined Chet Baker's road band, Feingold got the opportunity to photograph the jazz legend for his record label. It was a quiet and, for reasons no one could know at the time, chilling experience —all of which is reflected in the photograph included here. "We met in an

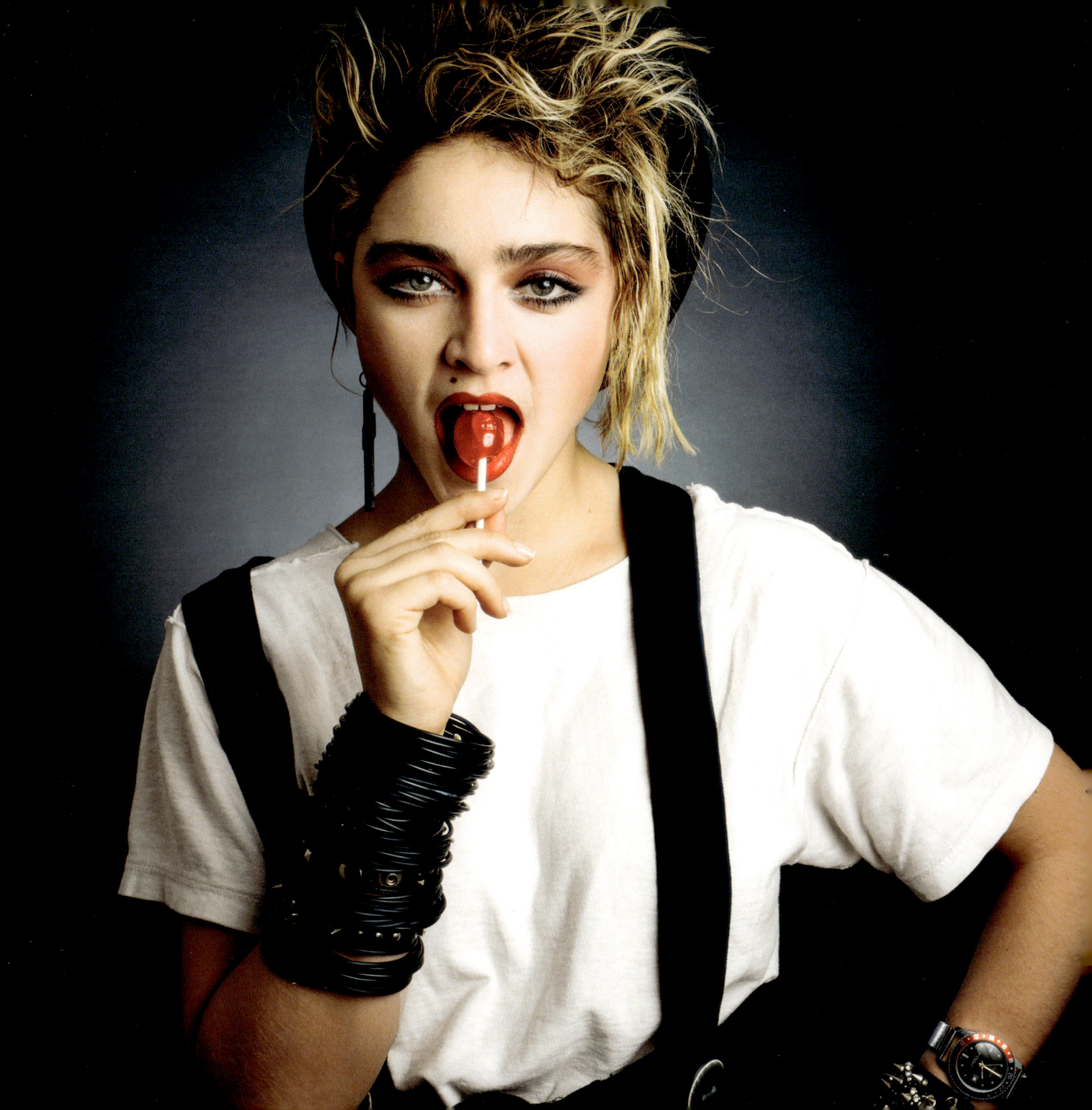

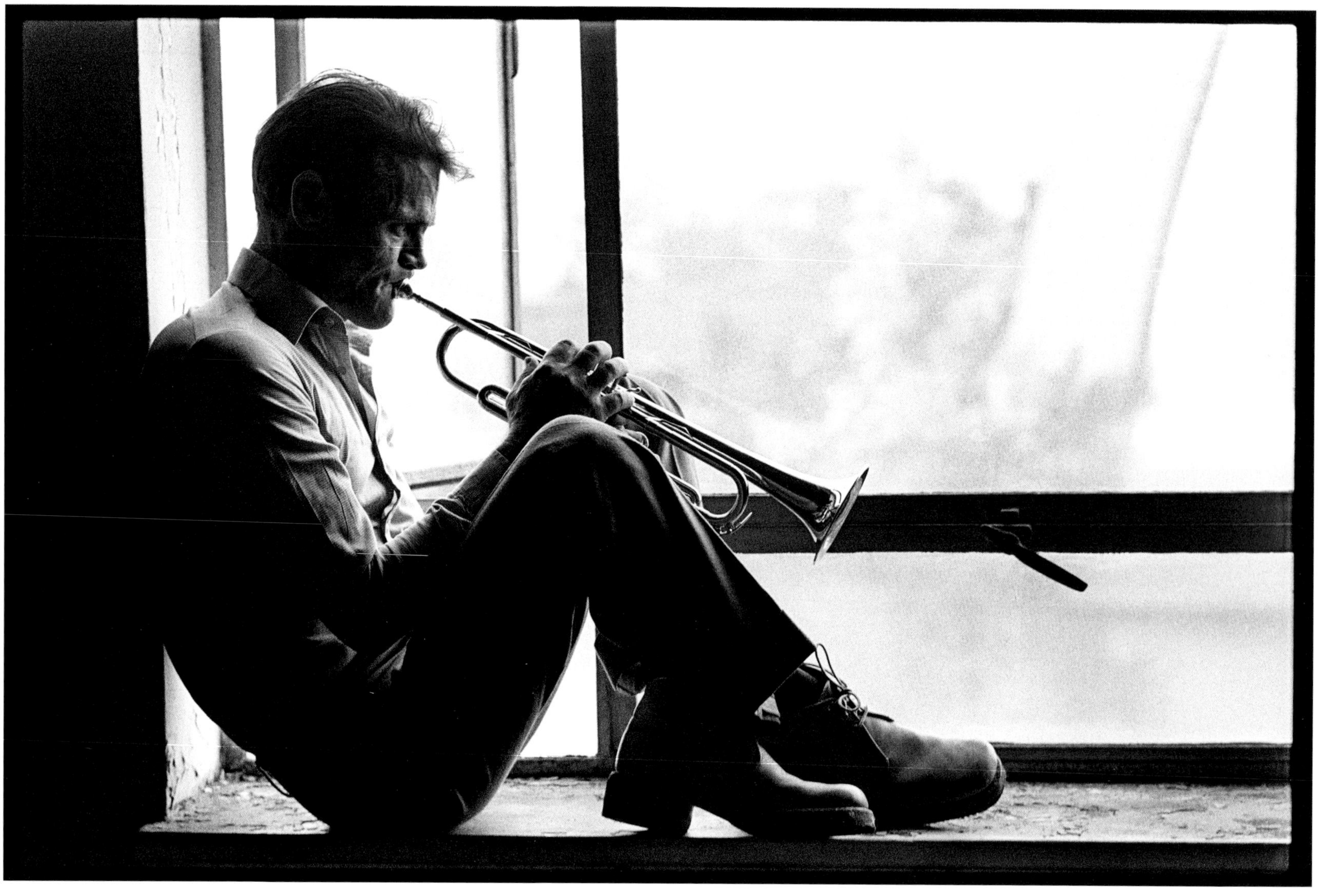

PREVIOUS PAGE: MADONNA, 1982; ABOVE: CHET BAKER, 1977

apartment at Ninety-sixth Street and the FDR Drive," Feingold recalls. "I'm not sure anyone was there but the two of us. We were both shy, so there was no conversation between us beyond, 'Could you sit here?' and 'Could you stand there?' I felt a certain fragility in him, a kind of sadness. The photos are haunting. For one of them, I asked him to sit on the window sill with his horn. Just about ten years later, he died in a presumed suicide after falling out a window."

On the strength of such compelling work, Feingold landed a prized photography internship at the *Village Voice*, where she got the opportunity to learn from notable editors like Fred McDarrah as well as from staff photographer Sylvia Plachy. Her breakthrough, however, came when she began to get assignments from *Musician*, a smart, serious, inventive music monthly that sought to give *Rolling Stone* a run for its money in the eighties and nineties. "*Musician* really broke ground," she says. "I was regularly shooting artists like David Byrne, Brian Eno, Steve Reich, Philip Glass, Laurie Anderson—everyone that *Rolling Stone* wasn't covering. We were kicking ass and having a ball!" Eventually, *Rolling Stone* came calling and offered Feingold a contract.

By this time, Feingold and her boyfriend had broken up and she was living in a tiny studio in the West Village. "I had a three-hundred-and-fifty-square-foot apartment, and everything in it folded up," she says, laughing. "My bed folded up. My kitchen table folded up. I made a photo studio out of that space, built a darkroom in my shower stall, and I shot everybody there. I always worked really small."

The room may have been small but the personalities were huge. Madonna arrived one day for a shoot for *Star Hits* magazine. "She came upstairs and the shoot probably lasted twenty minutes," Feingold says. "She had complete confidence—I'm not sure we even spoke. She just did her thing, took one of the lollipops I bought for the shoot, posed, and walked out." What remained behind is a definitive early portrait: sly, sensual, knowing. Madonna as a street-urchin Lolita with a physical knowledge of her quest for power, her eyes fixed squarely on the prize.

For the shoot with Bono, which also took place in her apartment, Feingold says, "I didn't know how to use strobes yet, so I bought a painter's reflector and put a hundred-watt bulb in there." It's as if the smallness of the space provided Bono with boundaries to break through, and he took the opportunity with characteristic élan.

The distinctive photo of Mick Jagger (on the cover) wrapping himself in his jacket, a rare depiction of his innate self-protectiveness, came about completely spontaneously. "During the shoot, one of my strobe lights exploded and I had to tend to it," she recalls. "When I turned back around, I saw him like that and quickly shot off one frame."

Equally spontaneous is the shot of Paul Shaffer lying on a divan on the streets of New York City, outside a restaurant serendipitously named Paul's Lounge. "He was in Gramercy Park and I was supposed to meet him there," Feingold recalls. "On my way I walked by Paul's Lounge. A few doors past that was an antique store. I ran in, quickly rented the lounge chair, and dragged it in front of the Lounge for a quick snap. It was like a jazz session, all improvised."

On the other end of the conceptual spectrum, Feingold found the sweetness and gentleness in Joey Ramone, a singer who was rarely shot with anything approaching this degree of beauty and sensitivity.

James Brown, meanwhile, looks as if he's about to hop on a bus, no doubt heading uptown (or maybe to the bridge, as his frequent demand that his band "Take me to the bridge!" would suggest), another shot that came about on the spur of the moment. "I was only permitted to shoot him in a conference room as he was being interviewed," she says. "I obviously wasn't allowed to talk to him during the interview. I got some okay shots there, but I wanted something more personal, so I waited in the hallway and then followed him out of the building and onto the street. When he turned around and smiled at me like that, I knew that was the moment."

For the shot of Cyndi Lauper walking down the street, Feingold instinctively knew that less would be more. "We had done the whole shoot in my studio, which by that time was in a larger space in SoHo, with all the makeup and the glam," she says. "But I loved what she had walked into the studio wearing, so when we were done, I asked if I could take a few shots of her out on the street." The result is a photograph that somehow seems lost in time, as if it could have been taken decades earlier, when the streets of the Lower East Side, as SoHo was then known, were filled with factories and young, hopeful, immigrant factory girls in search of a better life. Lauper's beauty and determination, her gaze in the distance as she walked on the cobblestones, echoes all that.

In addition, there are moments of genuine intimacy, like the photograph of Yoko Ono in her apartment at the Dakota, an Andy Warhol portrait of John Lennon hovering over her as she gazes into the distance. "She told me that no one had ever photographed her in that room before," Feingold says.

Guitarist Mark Knopfler, meanwhile, is caught in a private moment in a corridor backstage, having a smoke and collecting himself before a performance.

And the late Stevie Ray Vaughan, as explosive a blues player as any the past four decades have produced, seems eerily alone and isolated on a beach along the Hudson River, with all the grandeur of the downtown Manhattan skyline, including the monumental Twin Towers, behind him. His sidelong glance appears sincerely questioning, as if he's wondering how all those gigs in all those Texas roadhouses somehow brought him to this strange place.

Sincerity, in fact, is one of the hallmarks of Feingold's photographs. They're about coaxing out and seeing what others might not be able to see, not simply reproduction. The images in this book often express great wit and humor, of course—that's evident. But more prominent is Feingold's desire to set her subjects at ease and encourage them to feel vulnerable enough to give something to the camera—and ultimately to the viewer —that reflects who they are as people. Not as celebrities certainly, and not necessarily even as artists, but as people. Because these particular people are musicians, what they reveal often bears a rich relationship to their music—in the beauty and simplicity of their demeanor, in the dynamic between themselves and their settings, in the eloquence of their faces, in the charged visual energy of their movements, in the calm contemplation of their reflection, in the force and power of their eyes.

You leave these photos with a greater understanding of these musicians' gifts and their struggles, their passions, and the private peace they make with themselves—or try to—when no one else is there to notice or care. Except that, in these cases, someone was there.

That these pictures visually say far more about their subjects than they do about Feingold is her gift. Taken together, however, what they do ultimately reveal about her is her profound empathy; her ability to feel, understand, and communicate the lives of others.

"I learned from a very early age to try to figure out how other people were feeling," she says, "to find a way to make them feel comfortable and safe. After that, anything can happen."

And what happened, fortunately for us, is what you find in this extraordinary book.

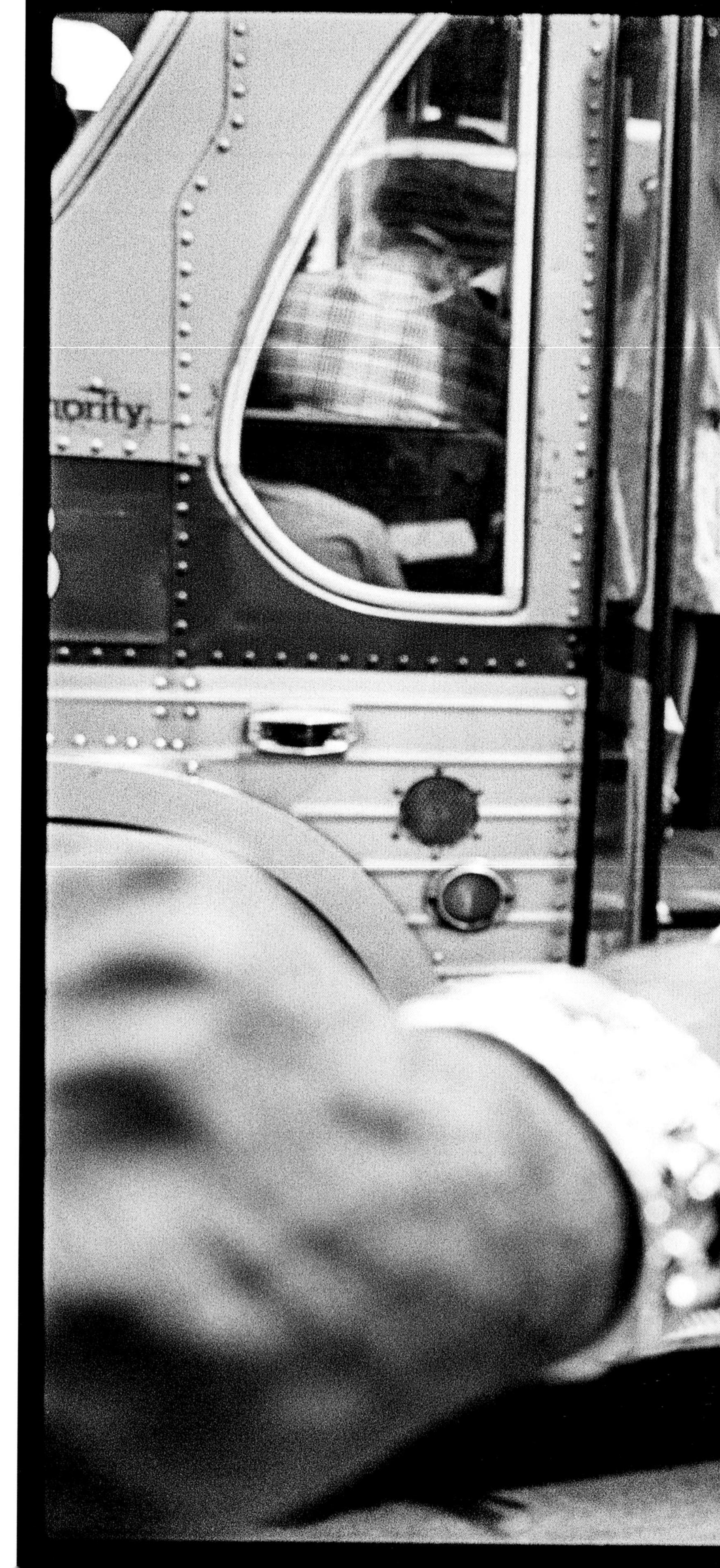

THIS SPREAD: JAMES BROWN, 1979
PAGE 10: KEITH RICHARDS, 2000; PAGE 11: YOKO ONO, 1990
PAGES 12–13: PRINCE, 1980

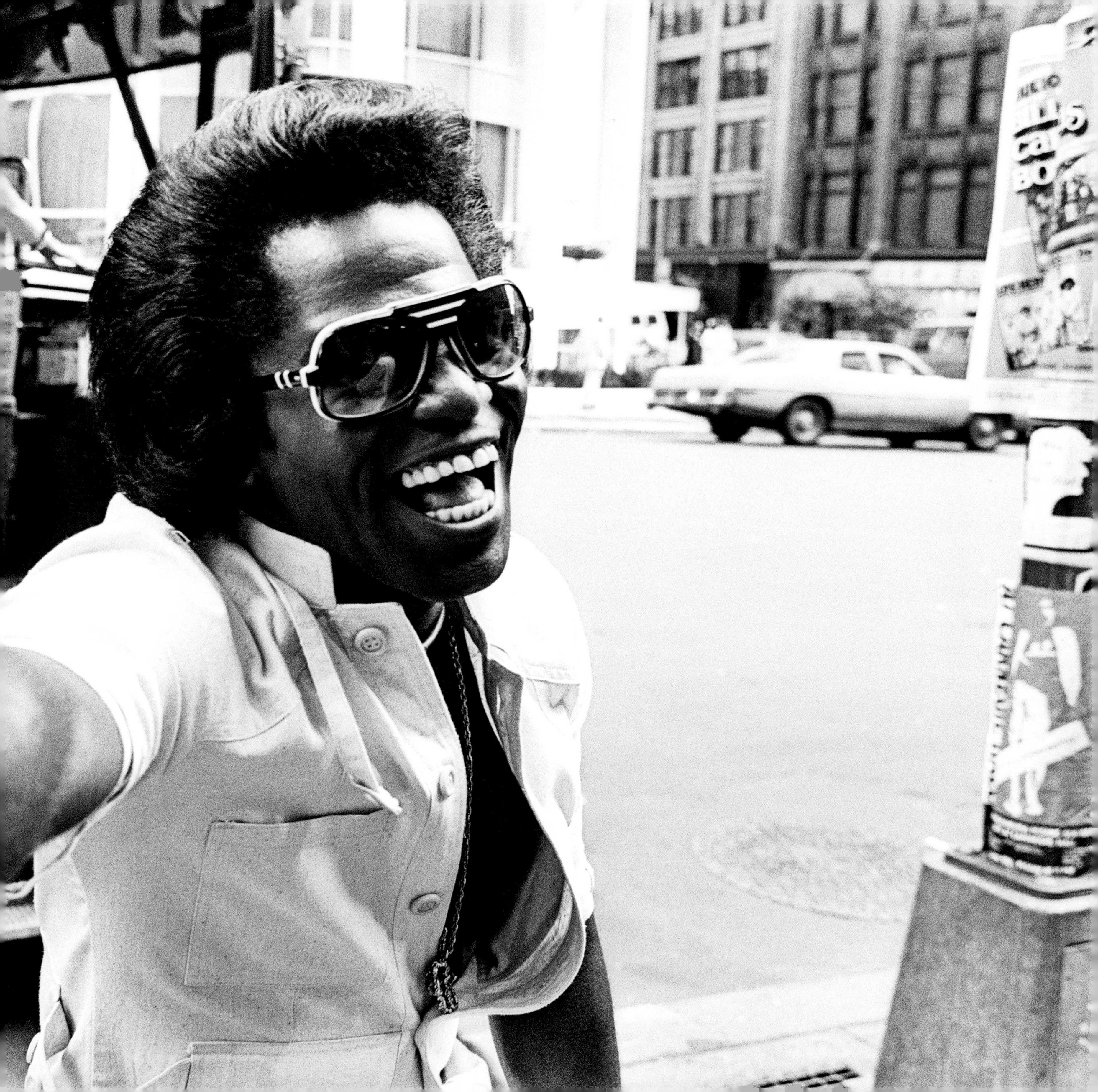

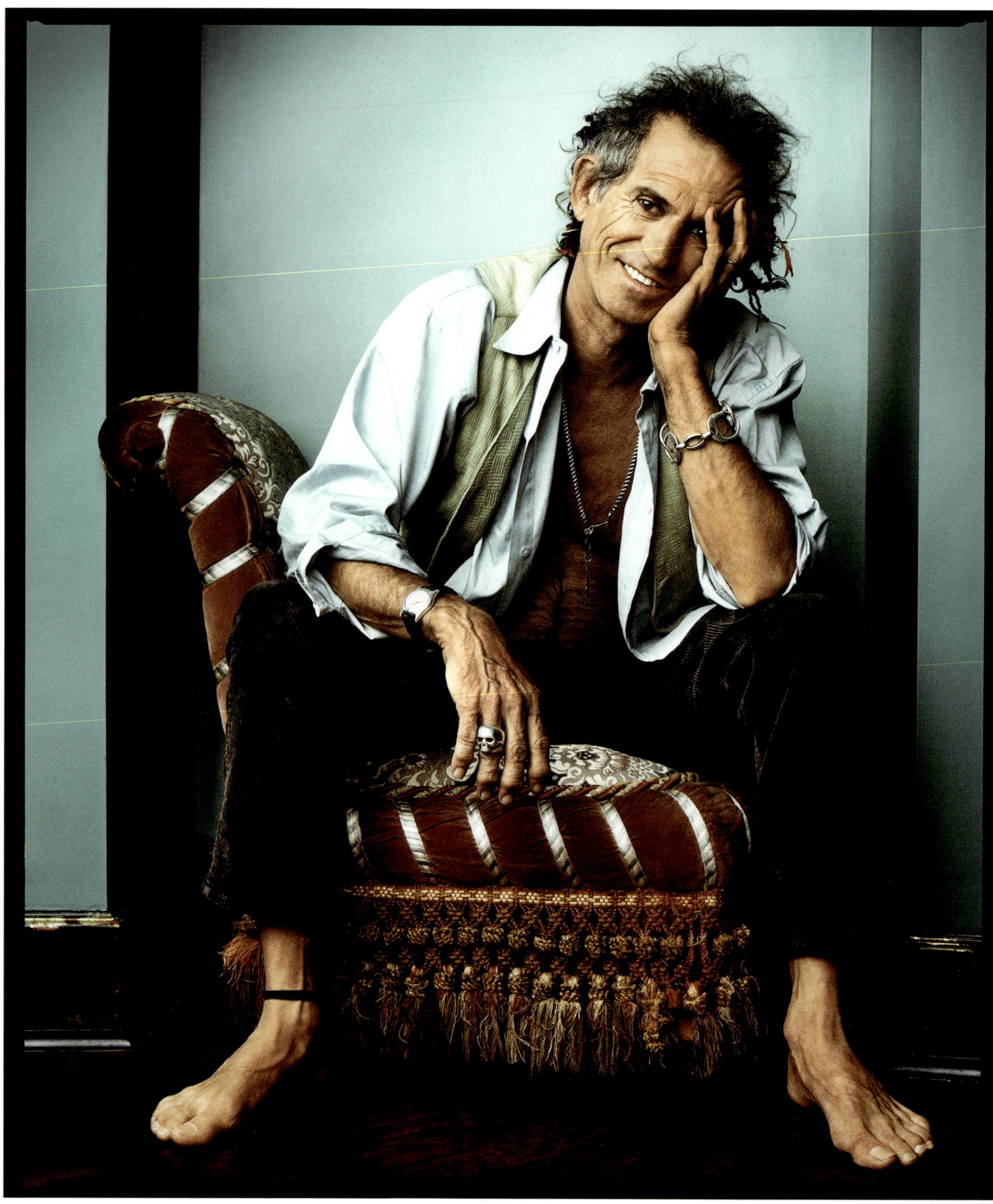

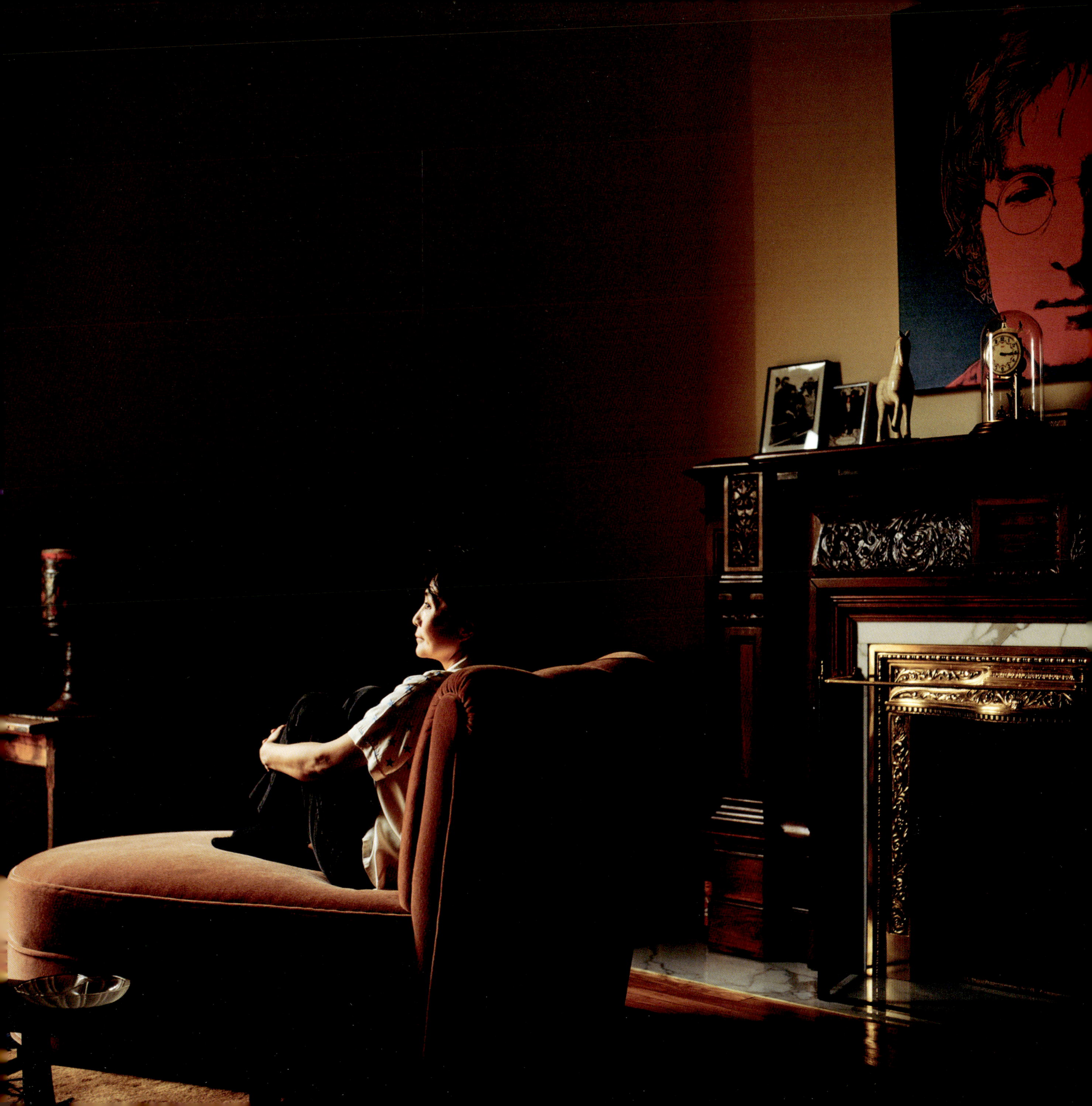

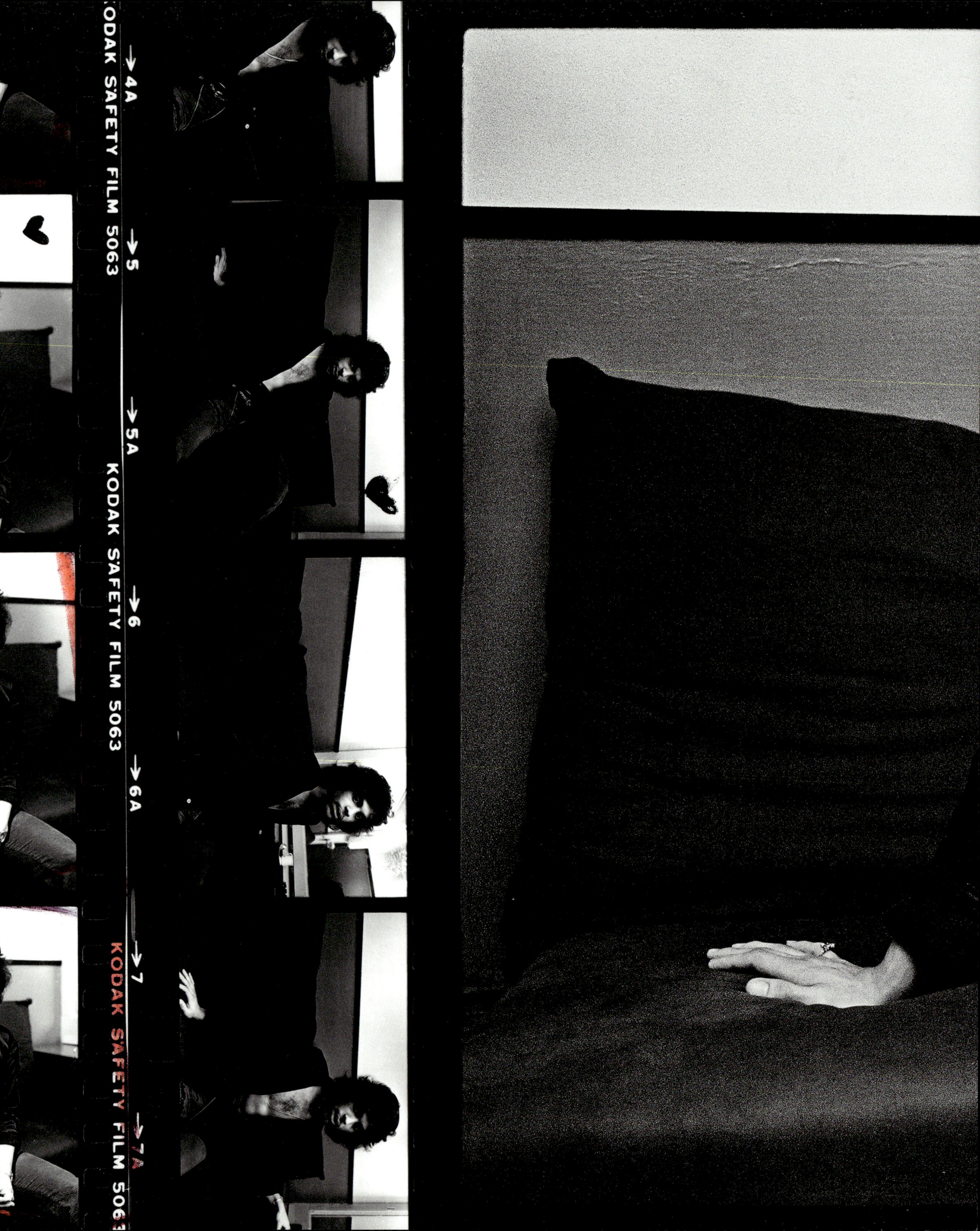

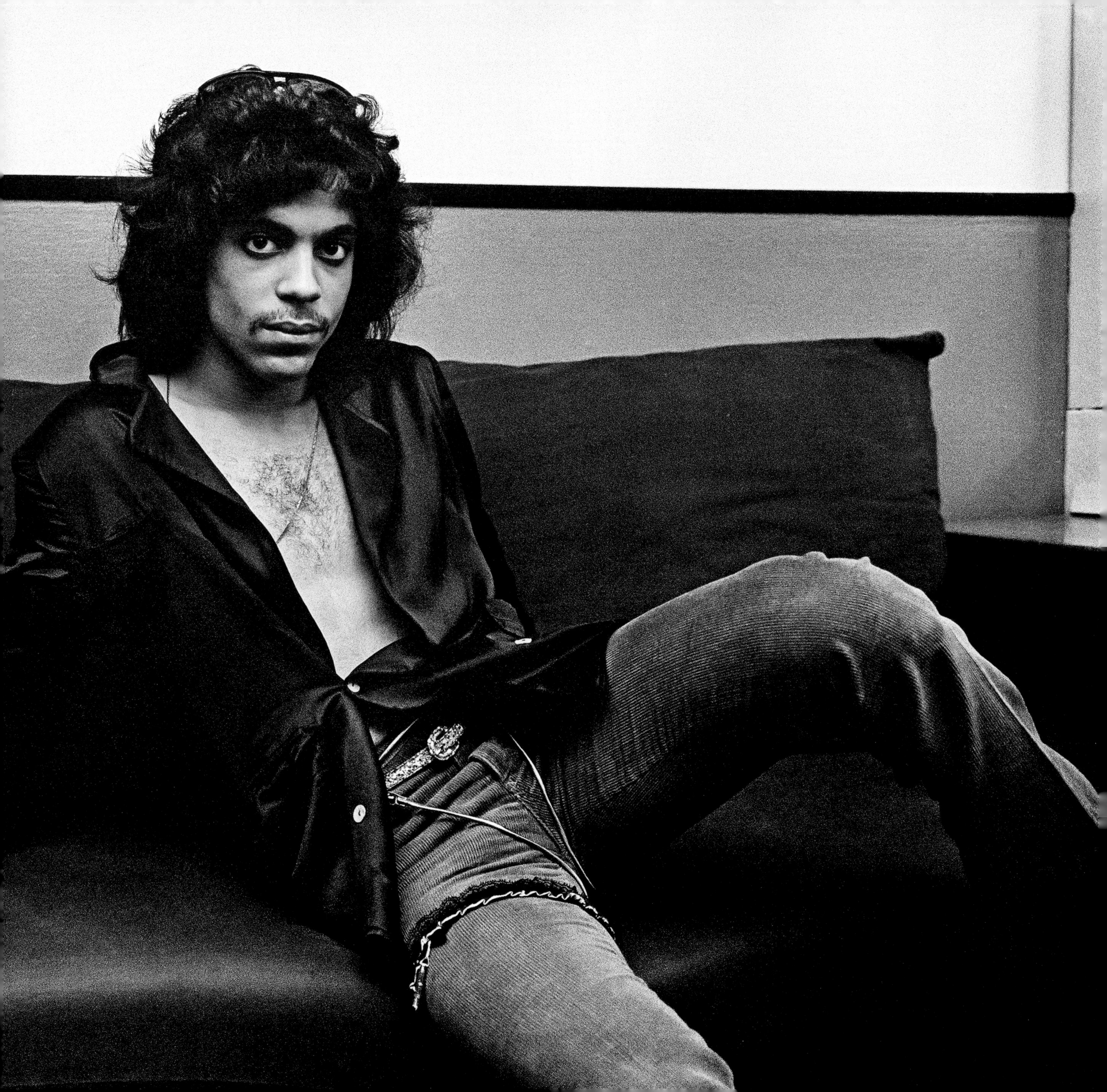

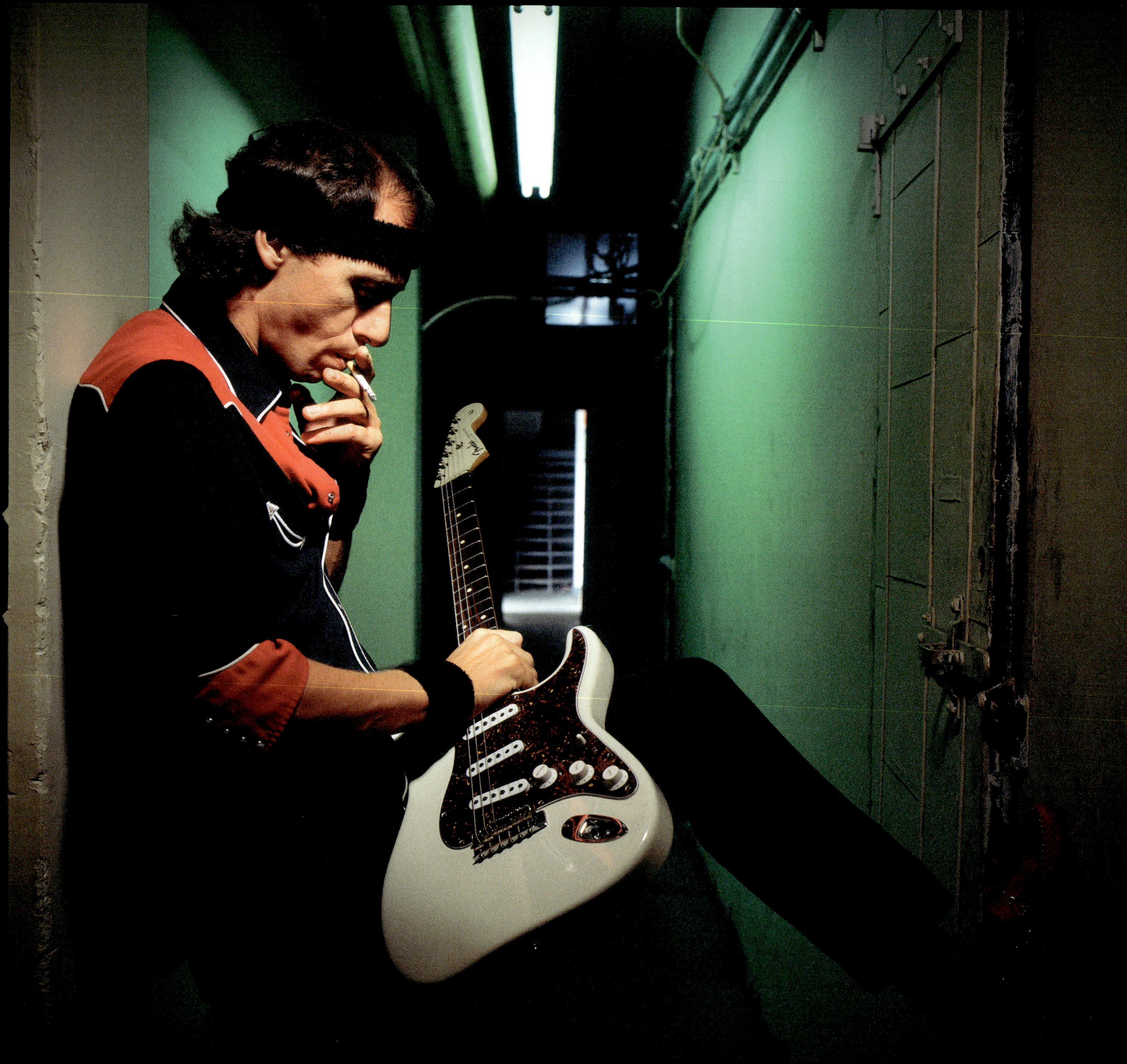

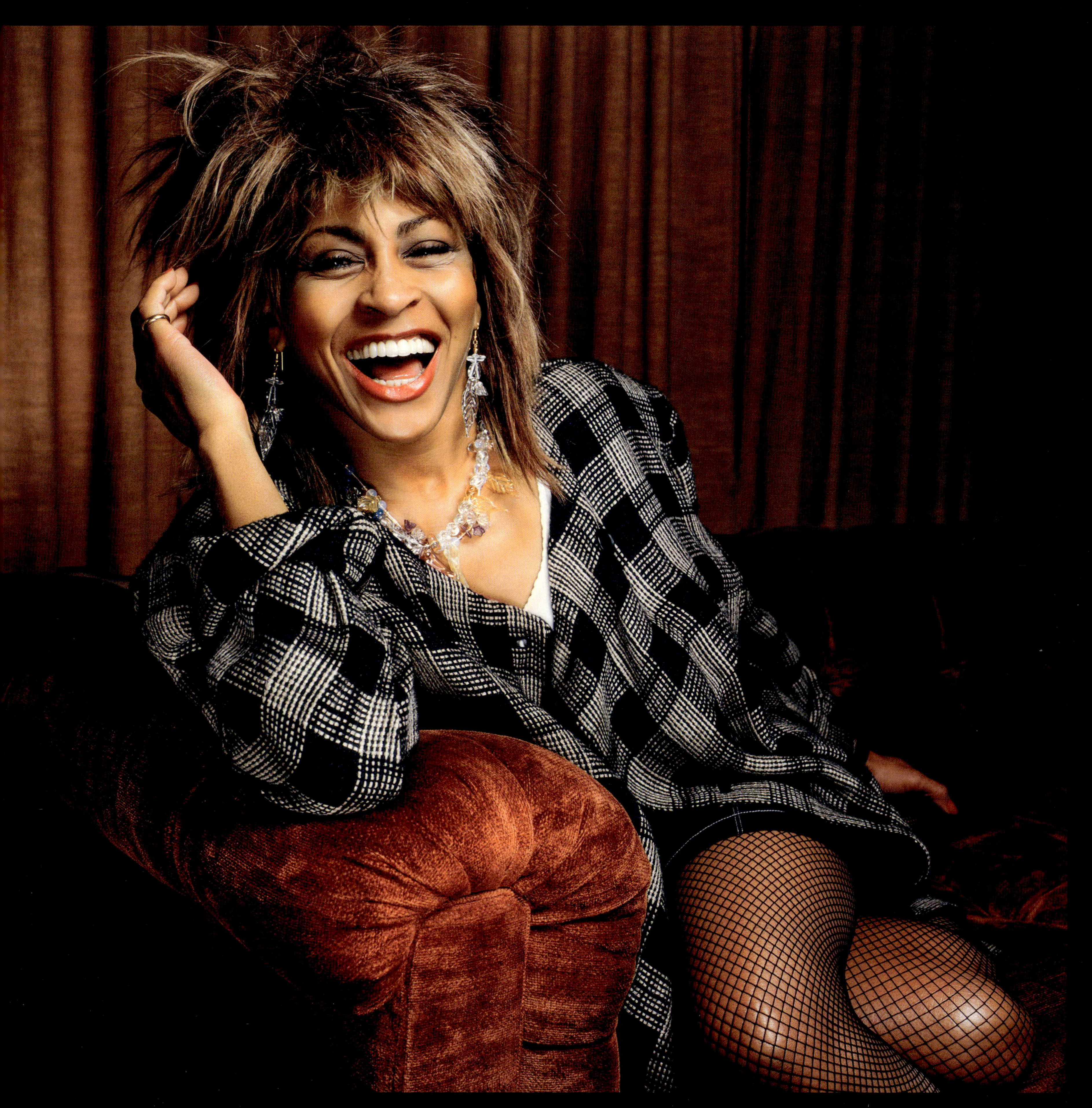

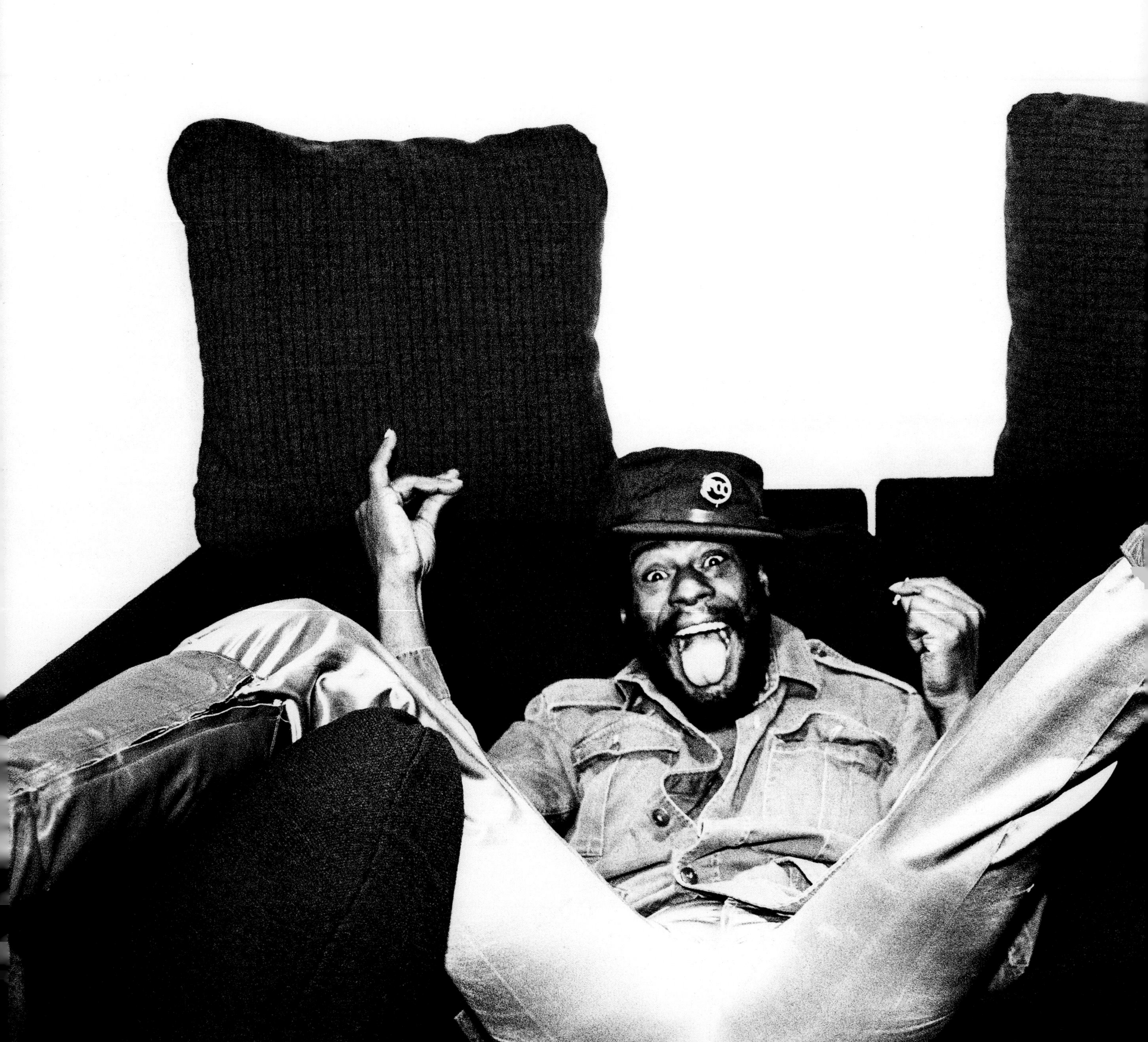

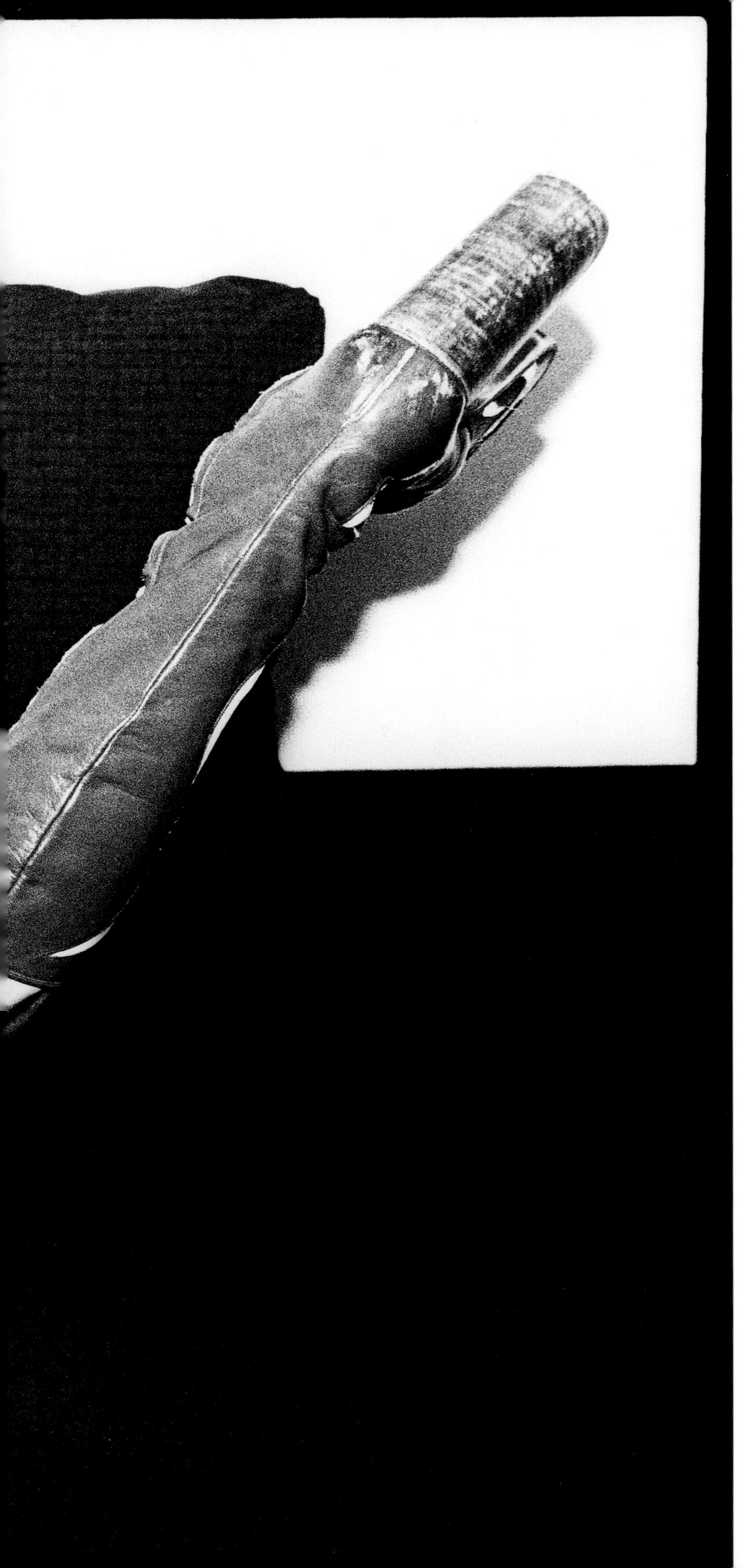

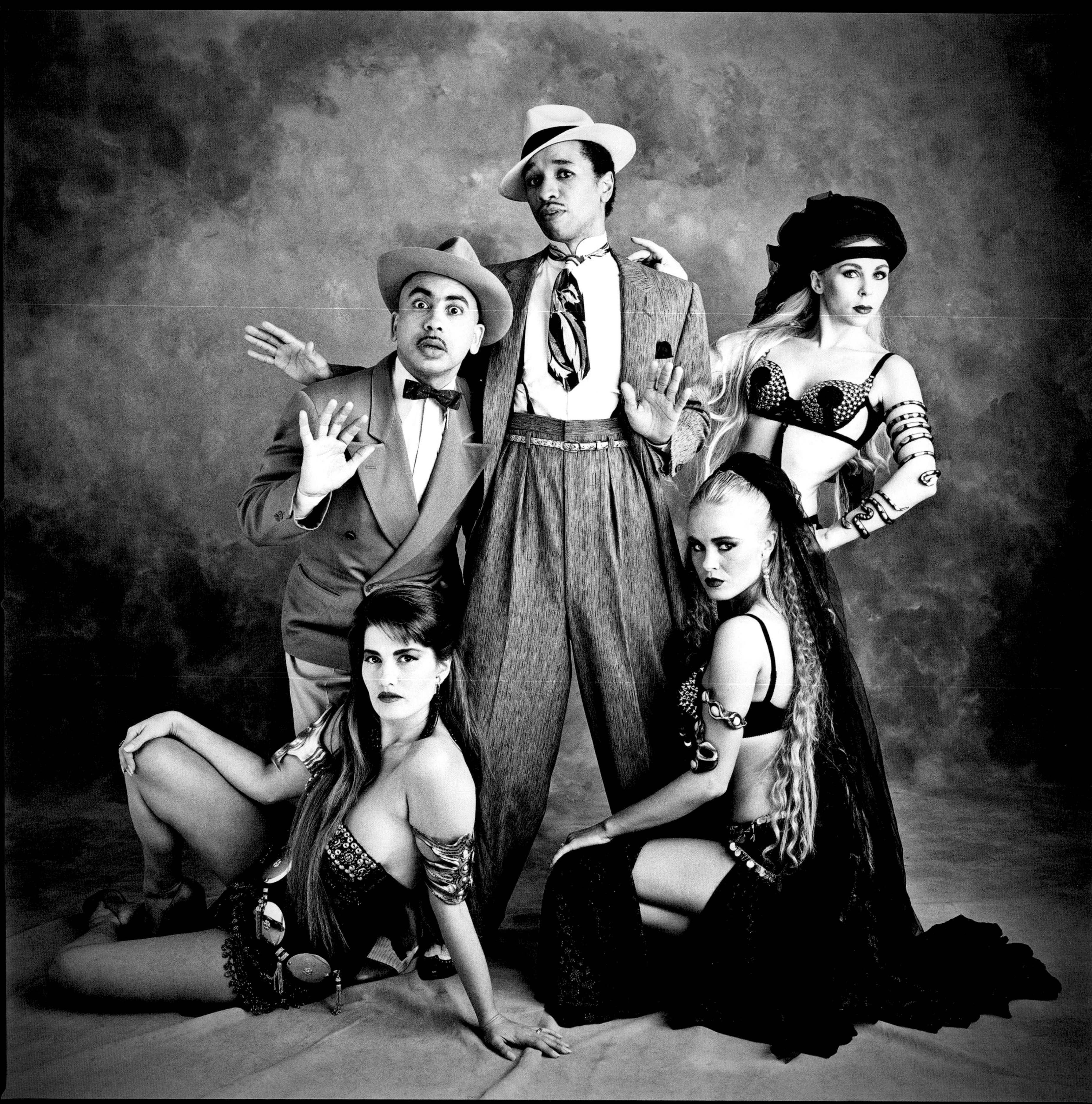

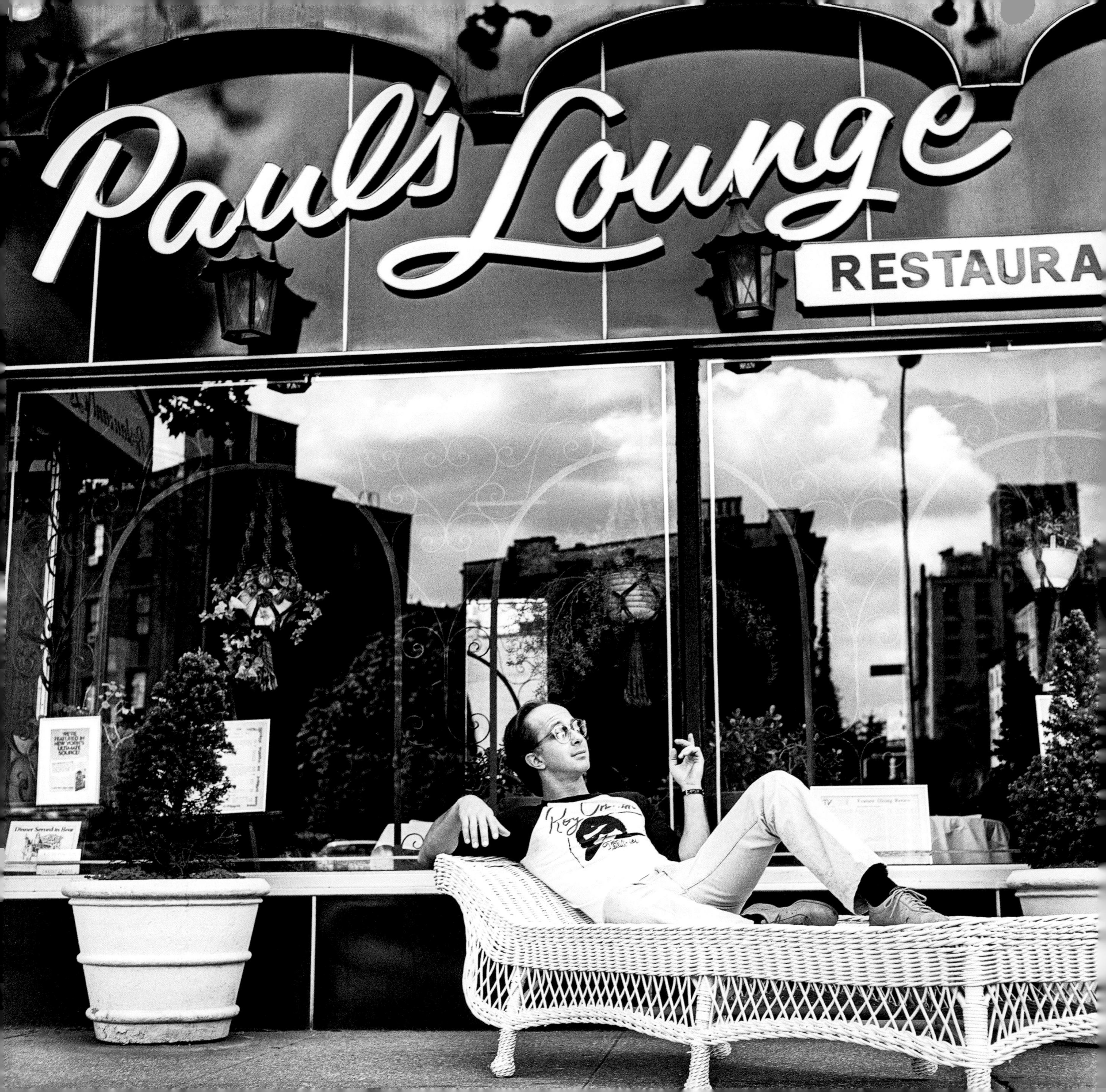

Paul's Lounge
RESTAURA

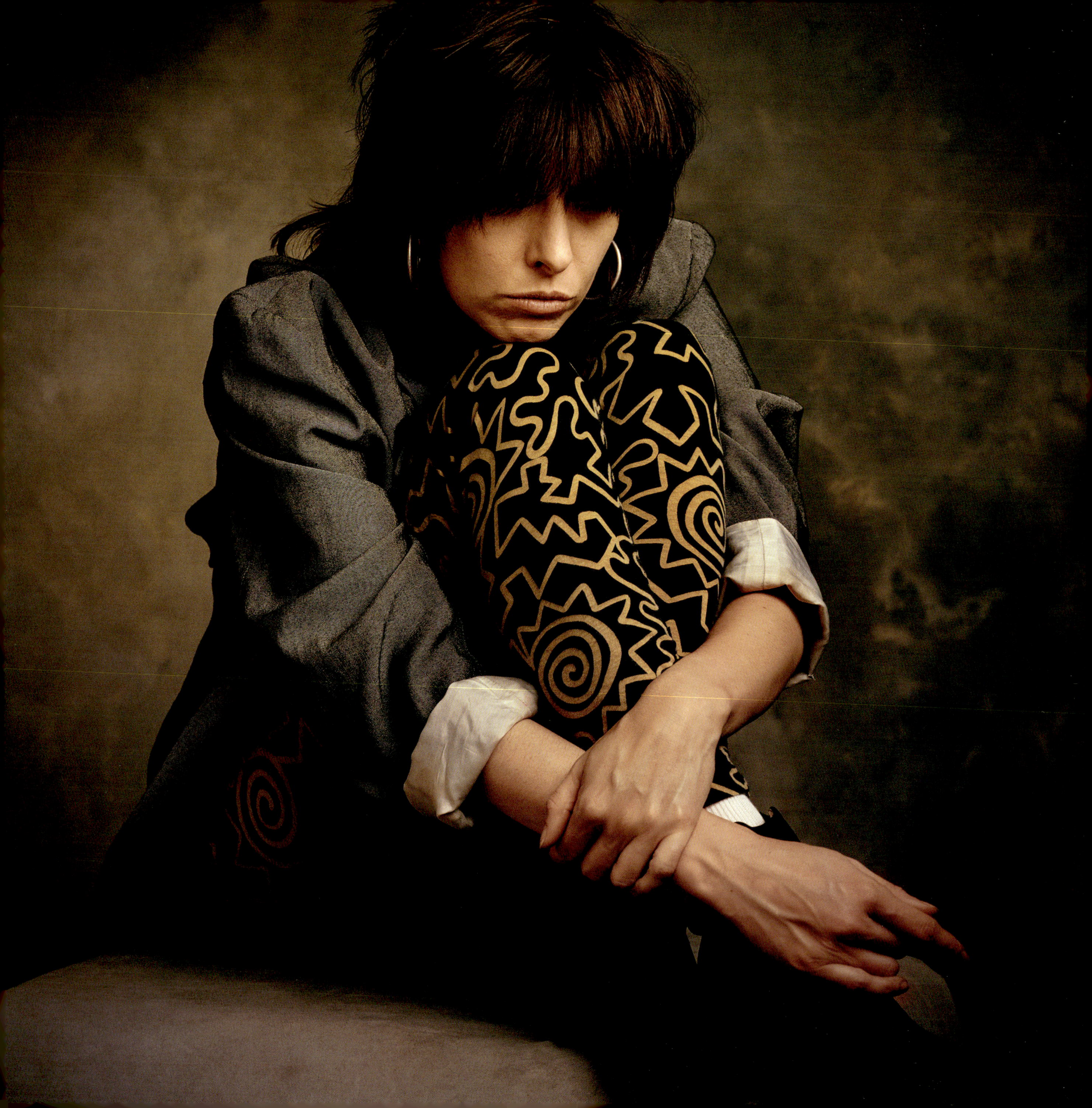

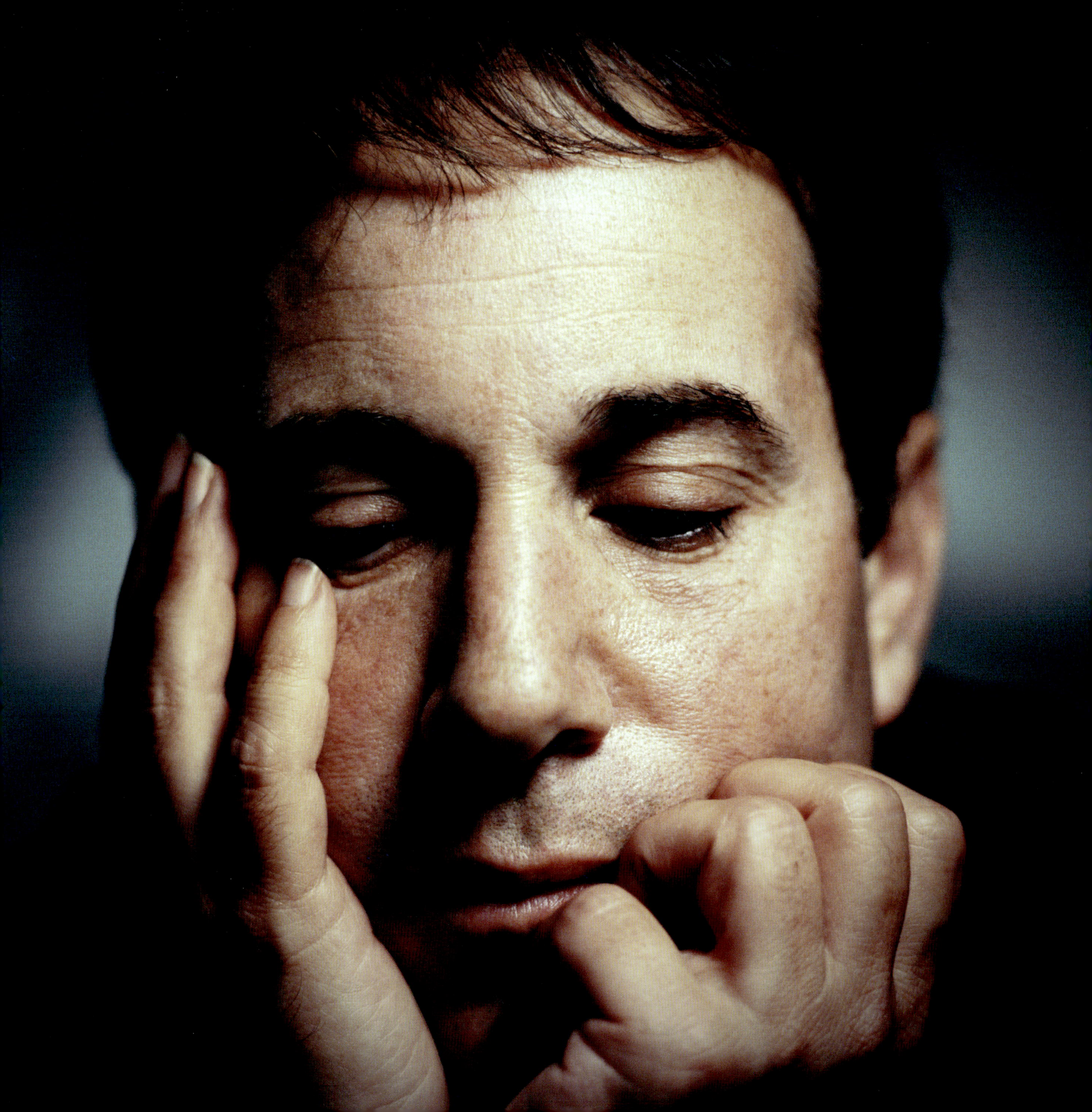

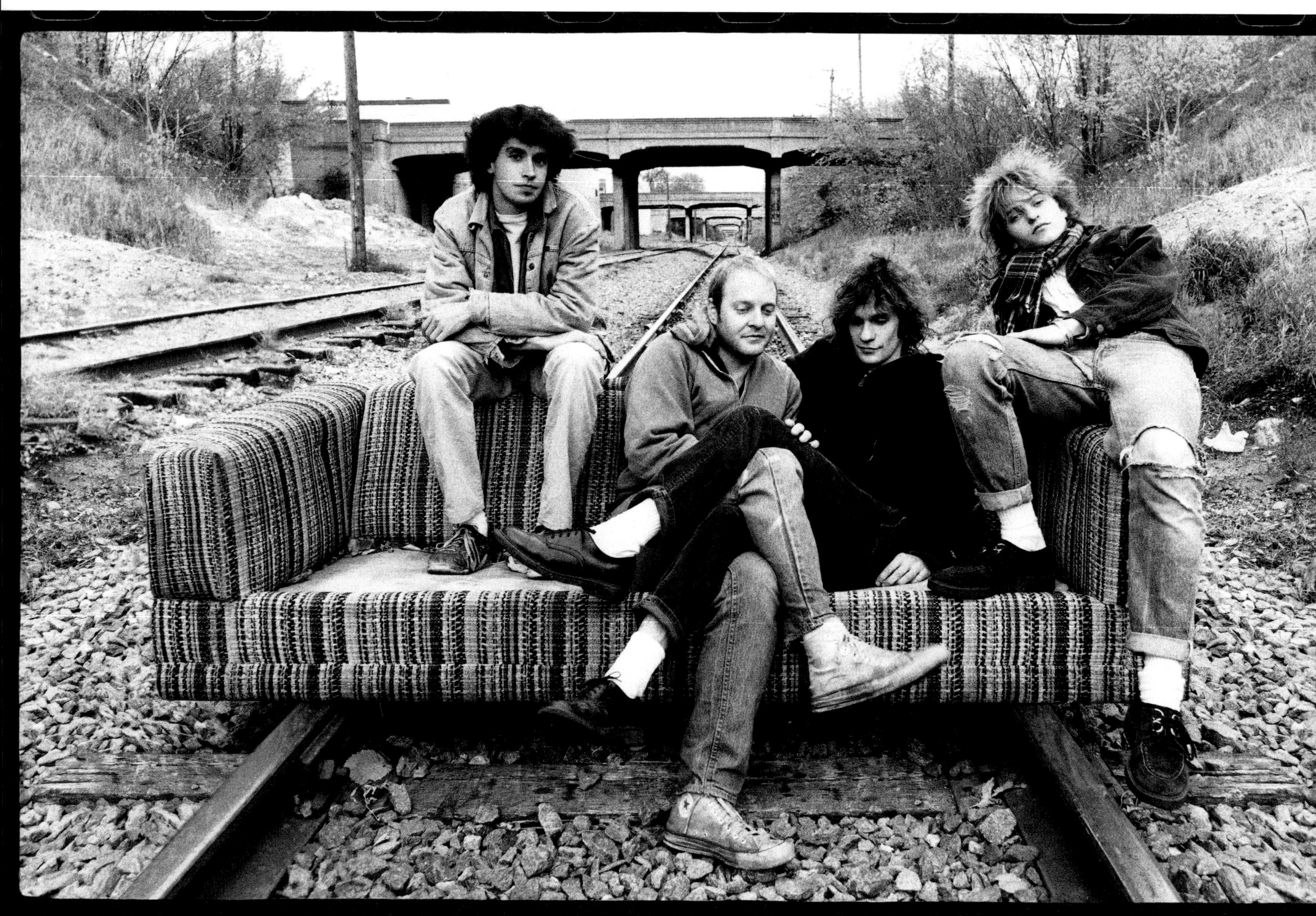

THIS PAGE: THE REPLACEMENTS, 1985;
OPPOSITE: JOHNNY COPELAND, 1981

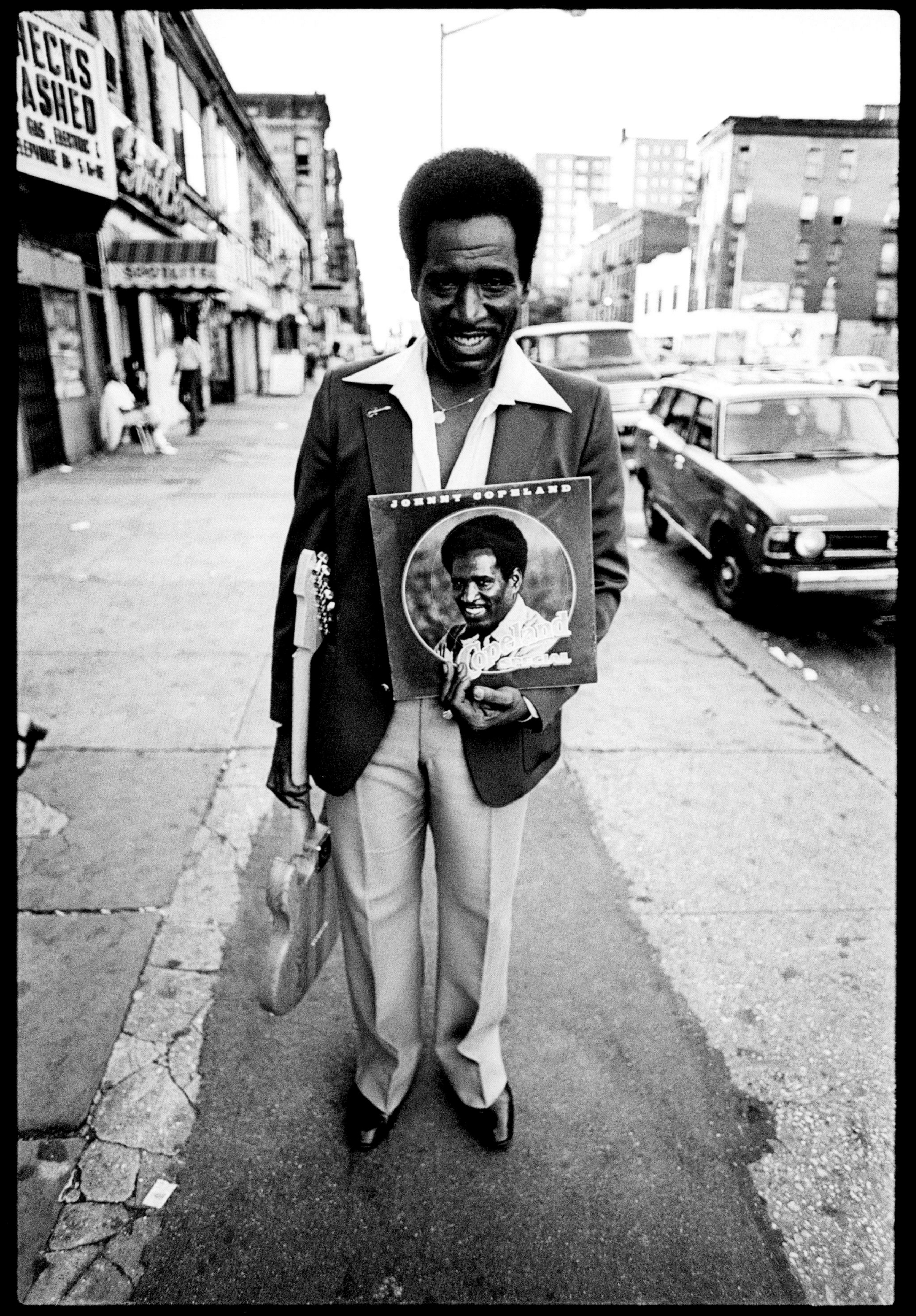
JOHNNY COPELAND
Copeland
SPECIAL

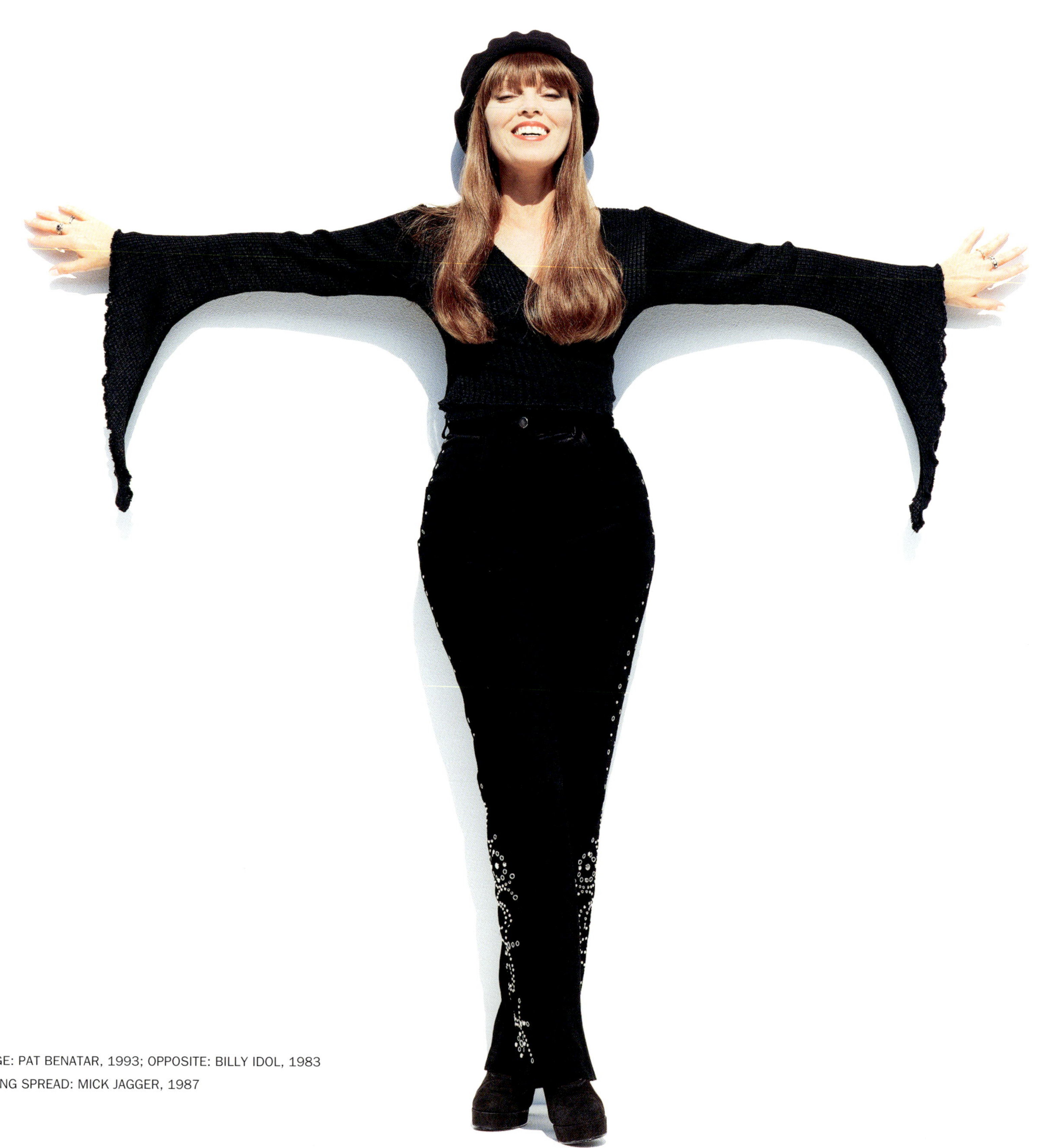

THIS PAGE: PAT BENATAR, 1993; OPPOSITE: BILLY IDOL, 1983
FOLLOWING SPREAD: MICK JAGGER, 1987

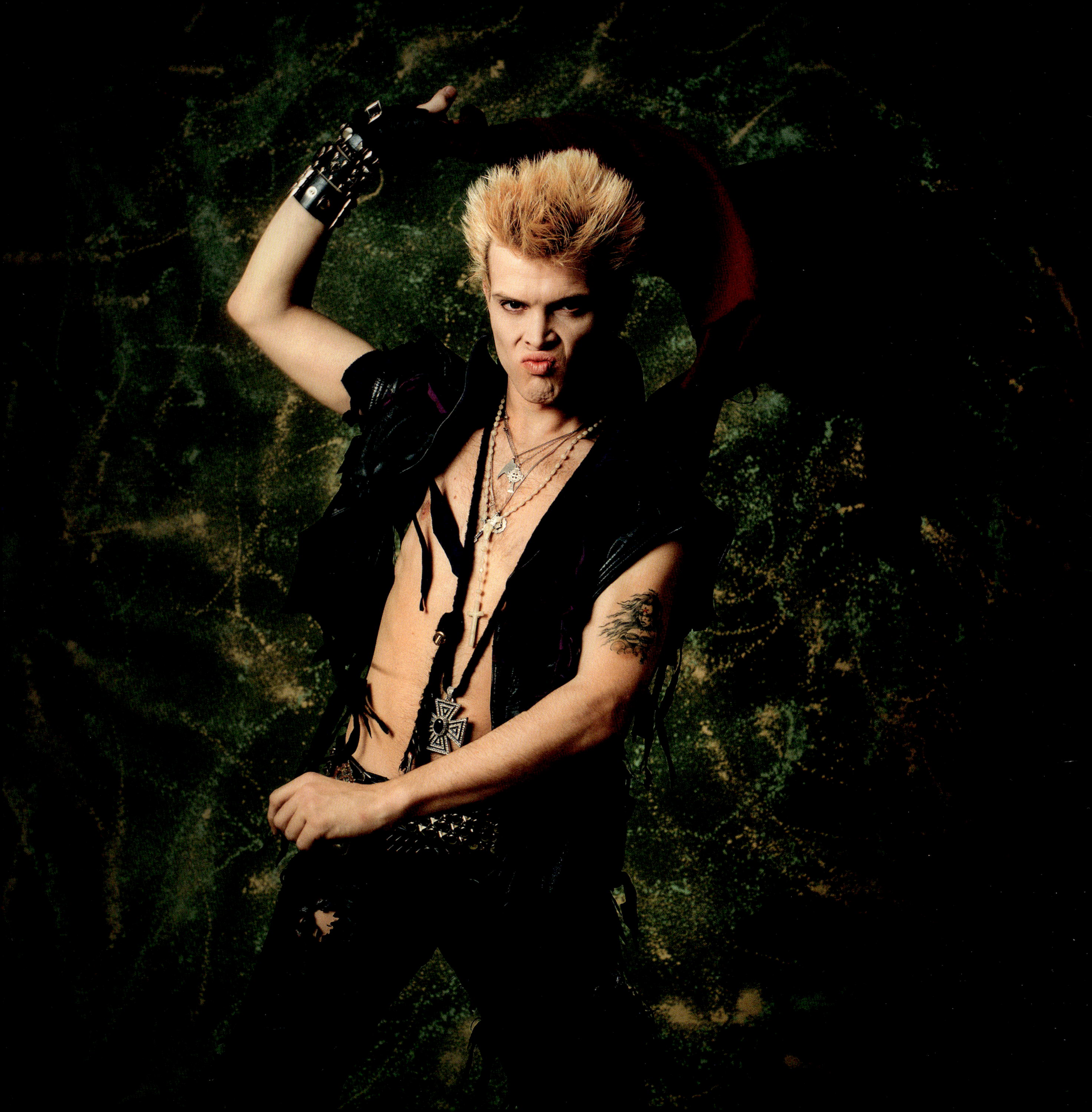

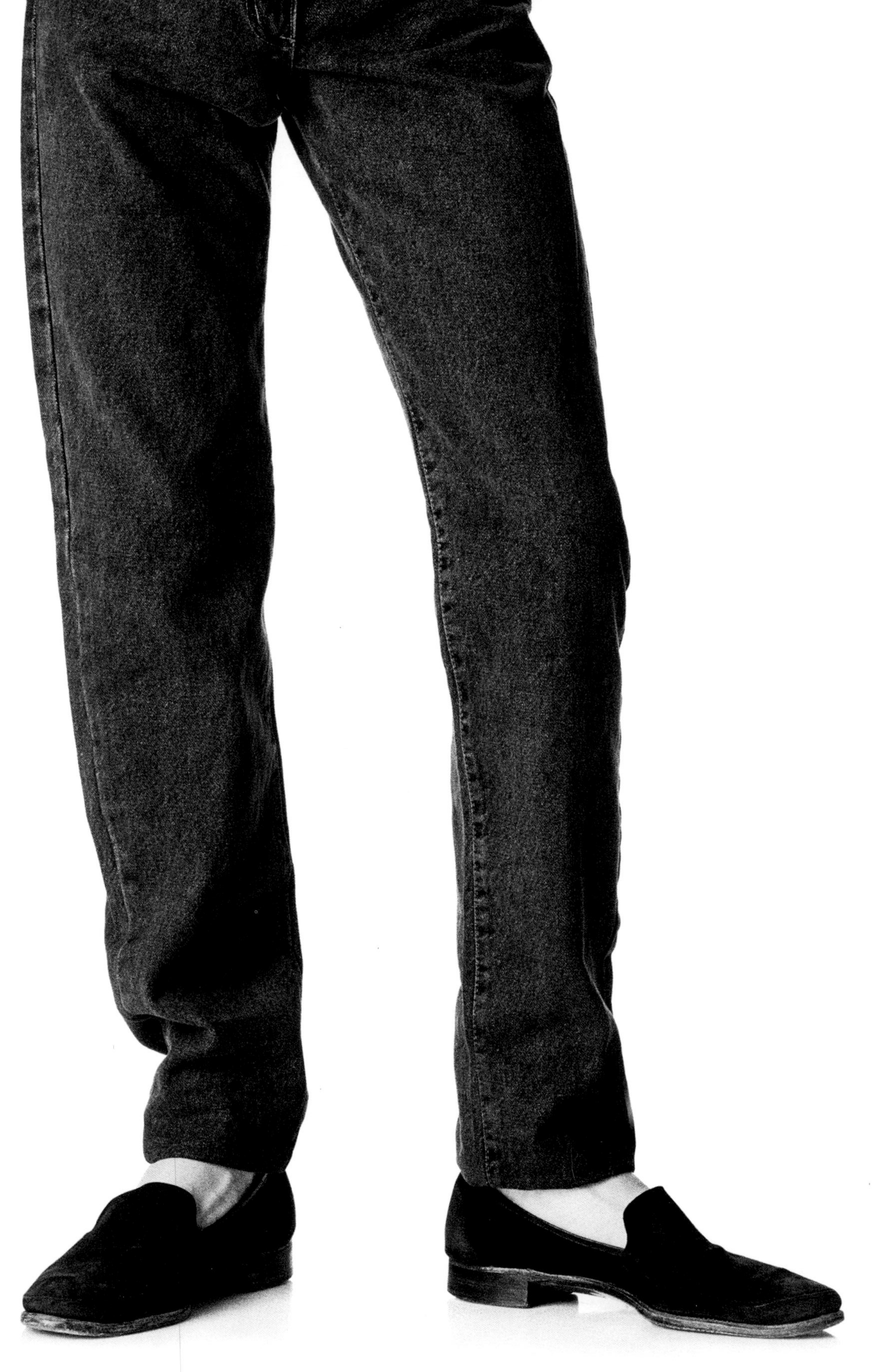

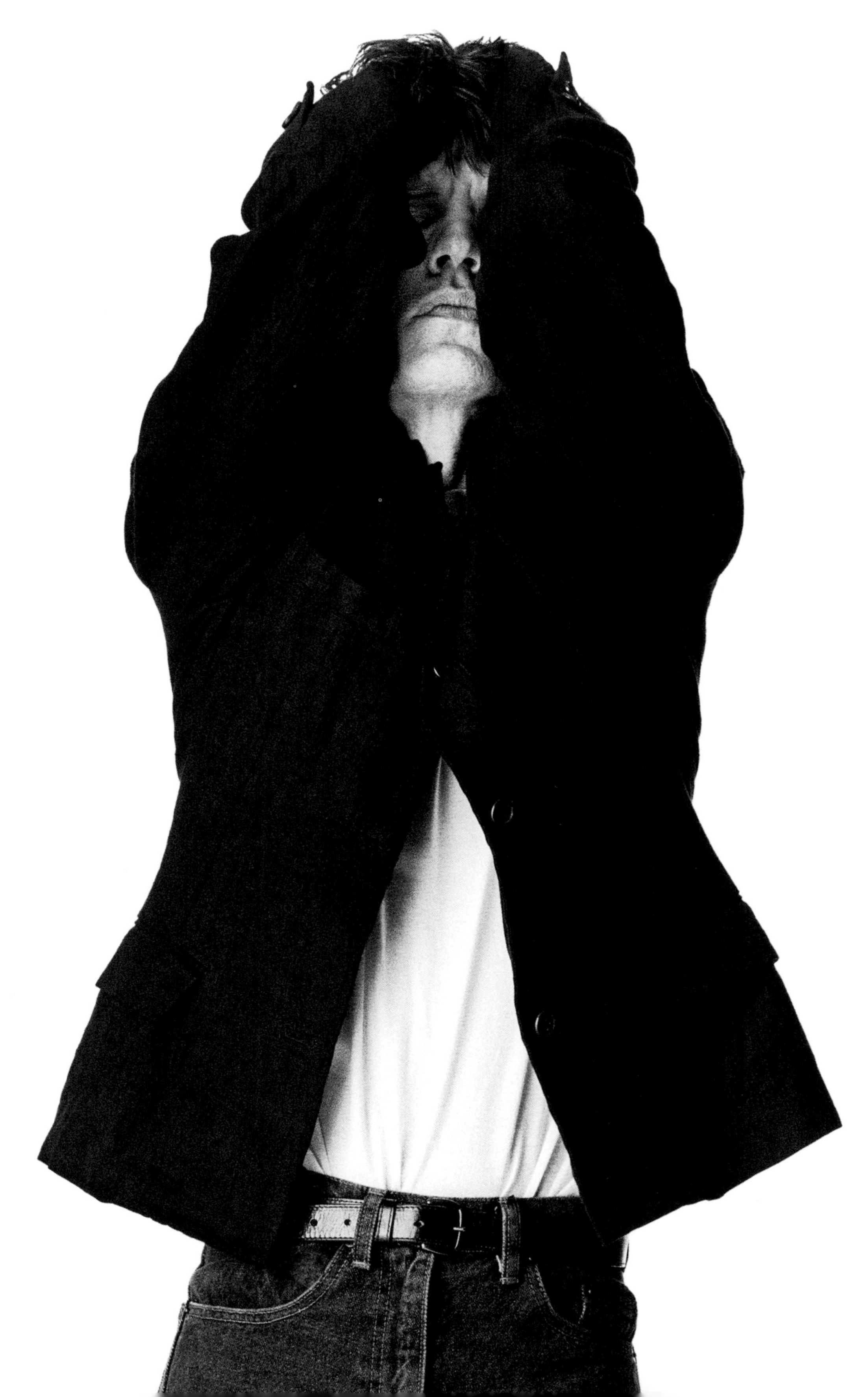

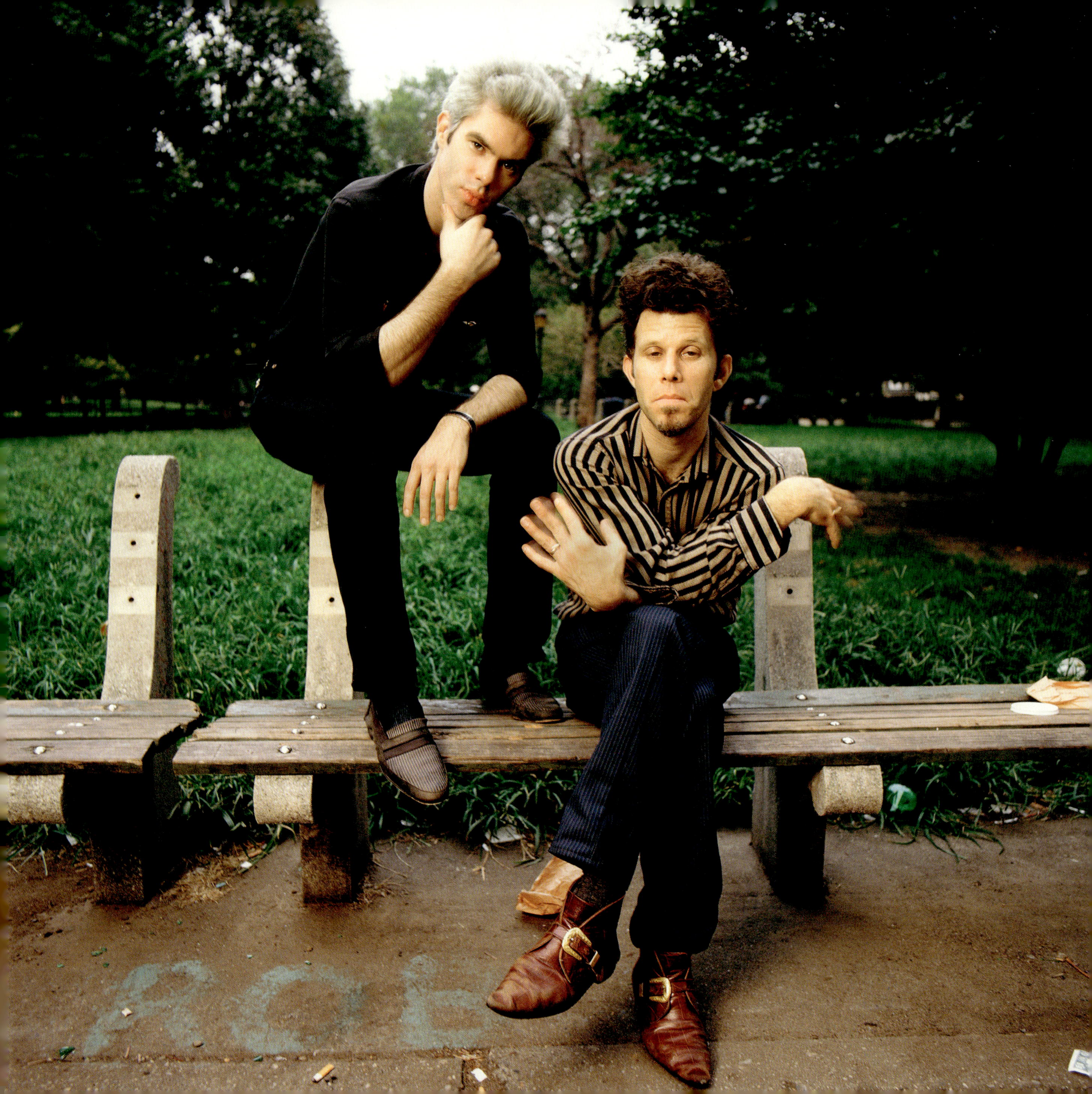

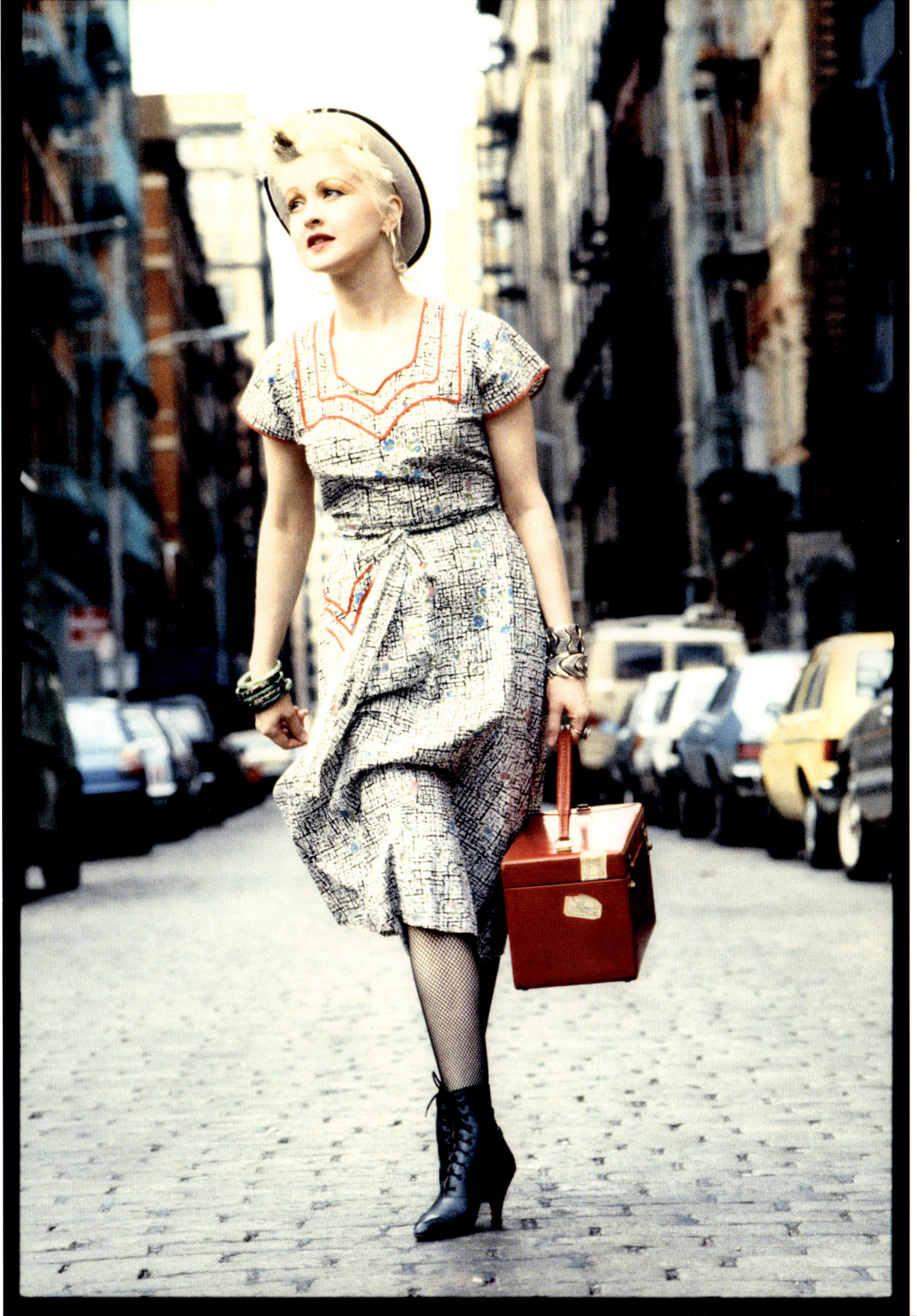

PAGE 28: TOM WAITS AND JIM JARMUSCH, 1985; PAGE 29: CYNDI LAUPER, 1988
OPPOSITE: DAVID BYRNE, 1983
PAGE 32: EDDIE VAN HALEN AND VALERIE BERTINELLI, 1985; PAGE 33: SPINAL TAP, 1984
PAGE 34: PHARRELL WILLIAMS, 2003; PAGE 35: JOEY RAMONE, 1983

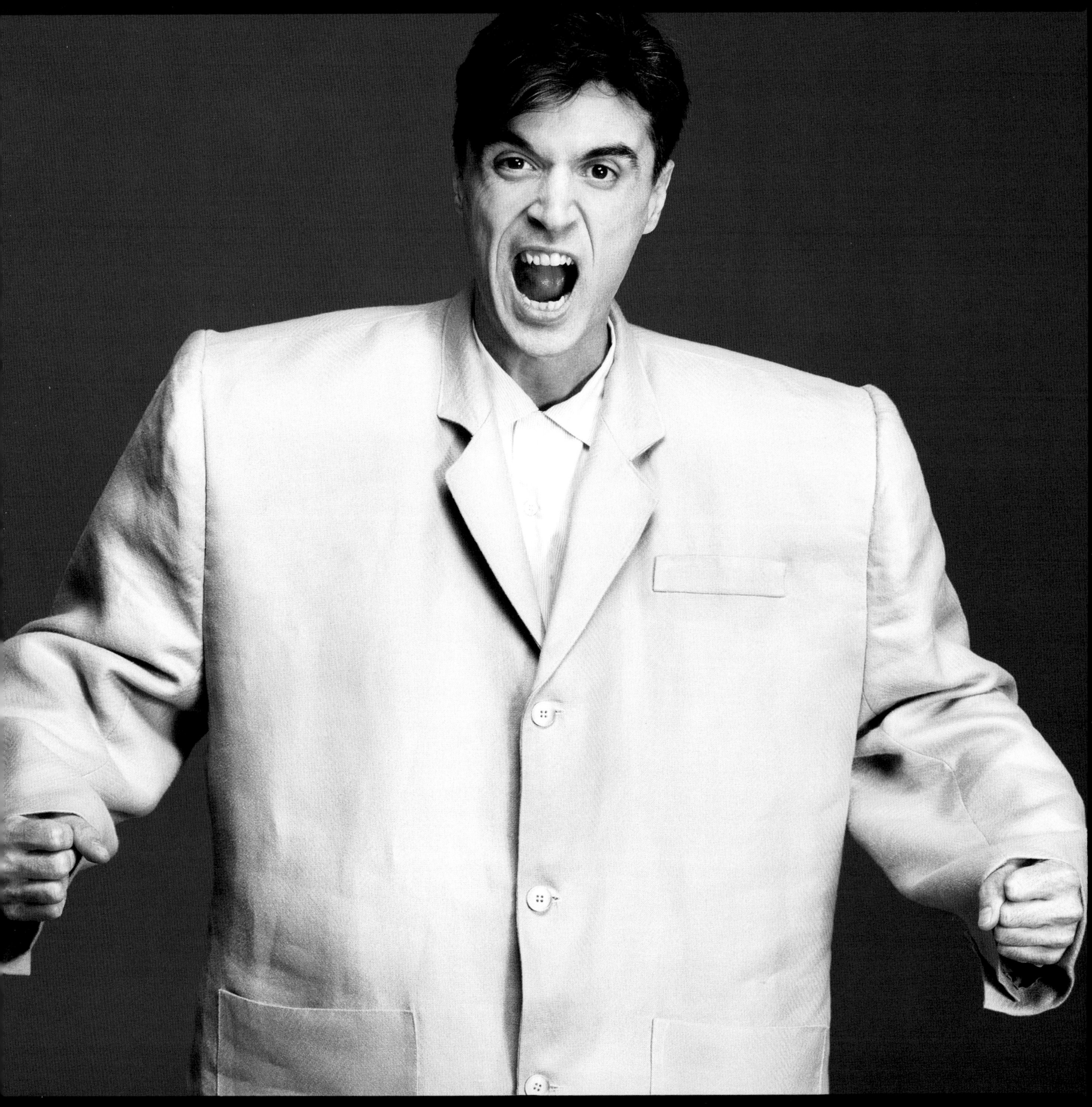

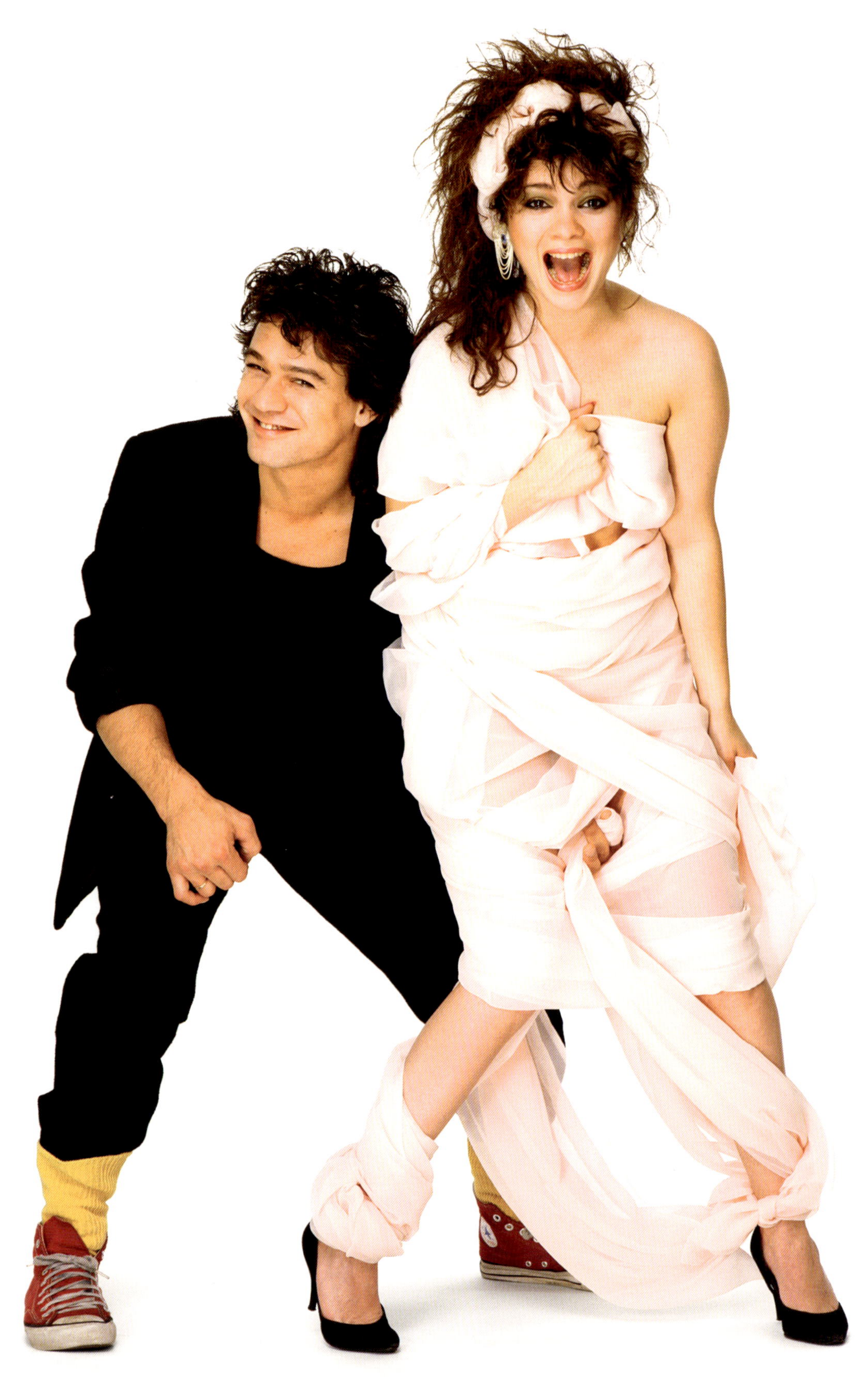

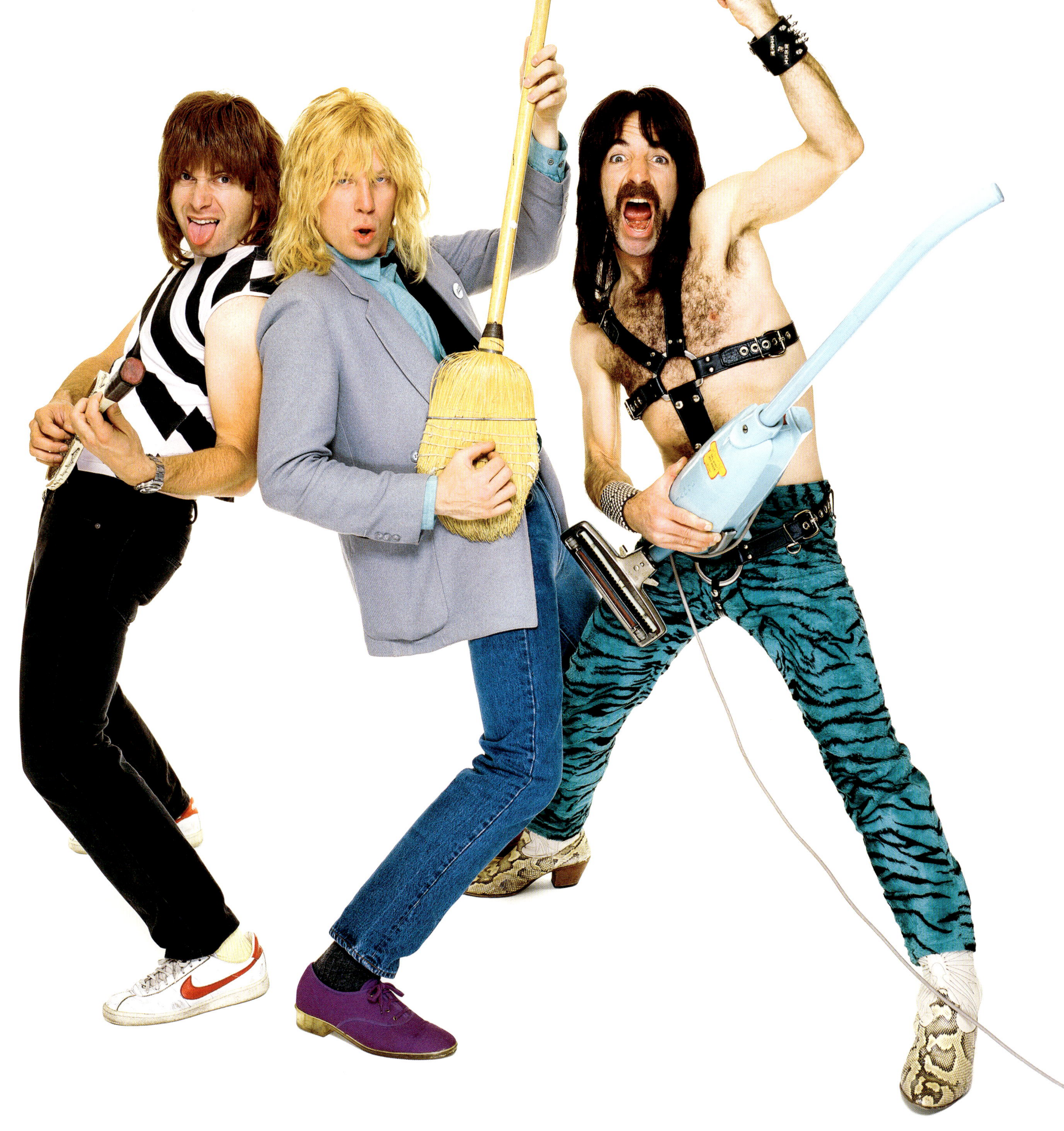

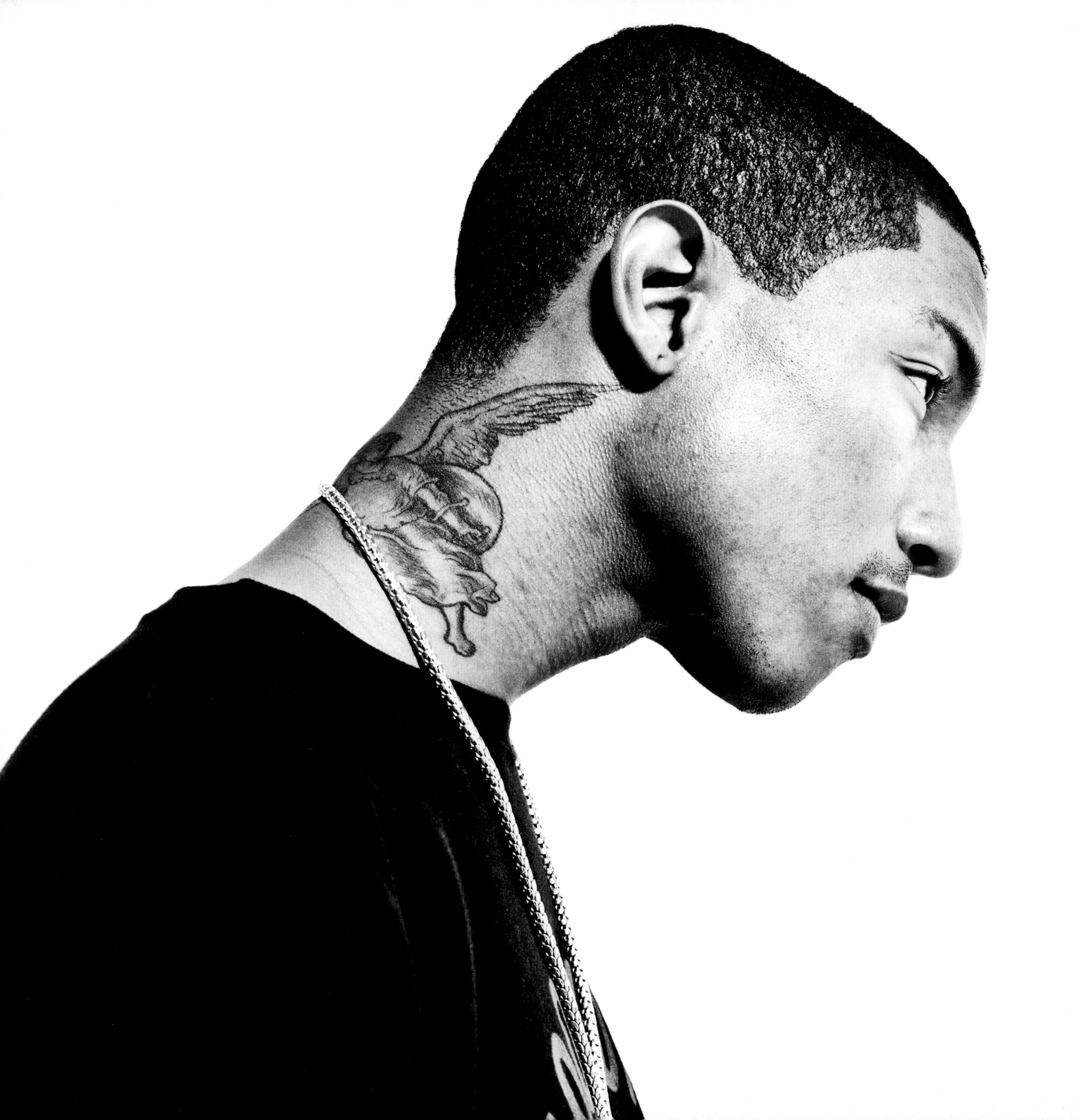

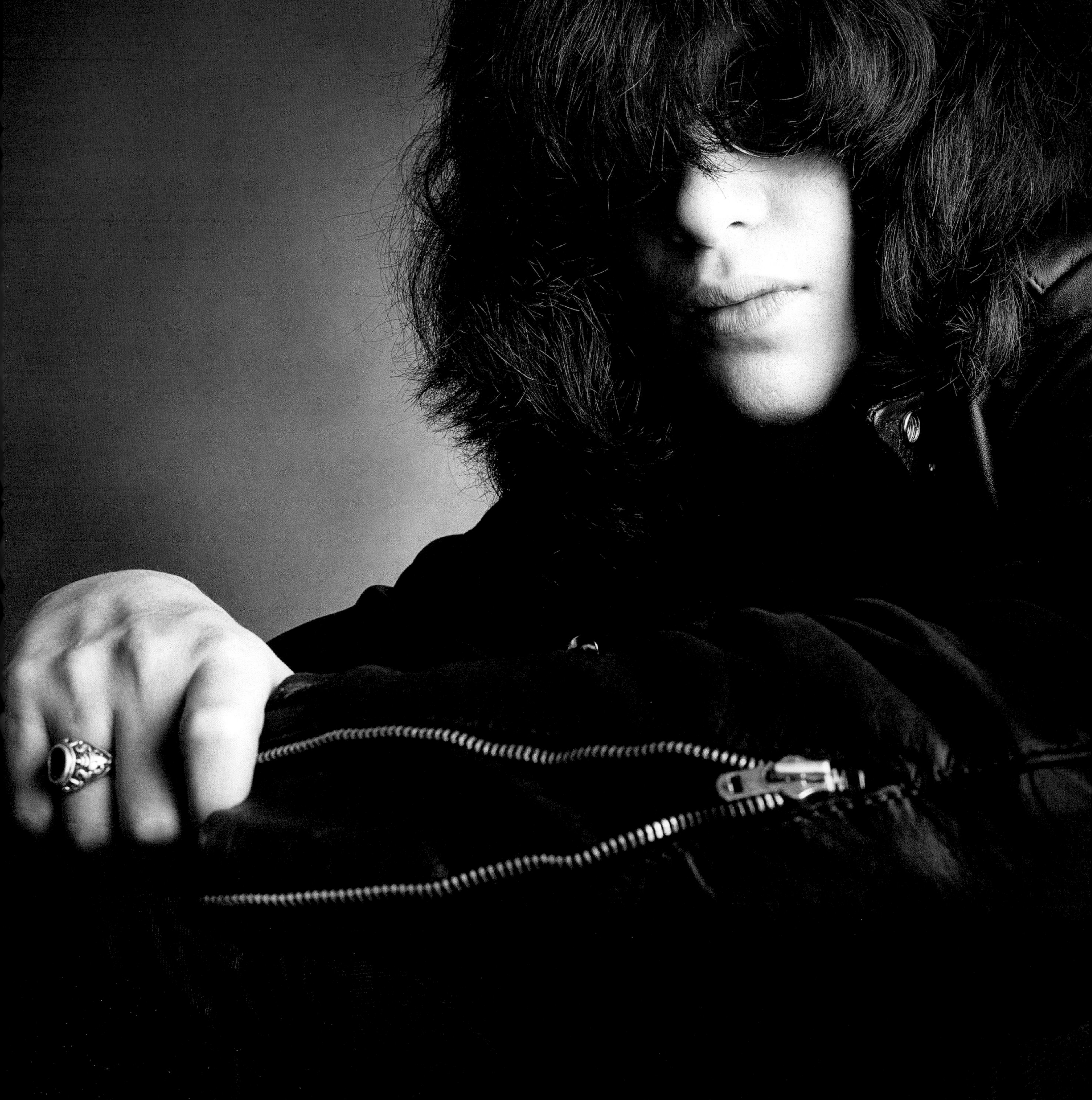

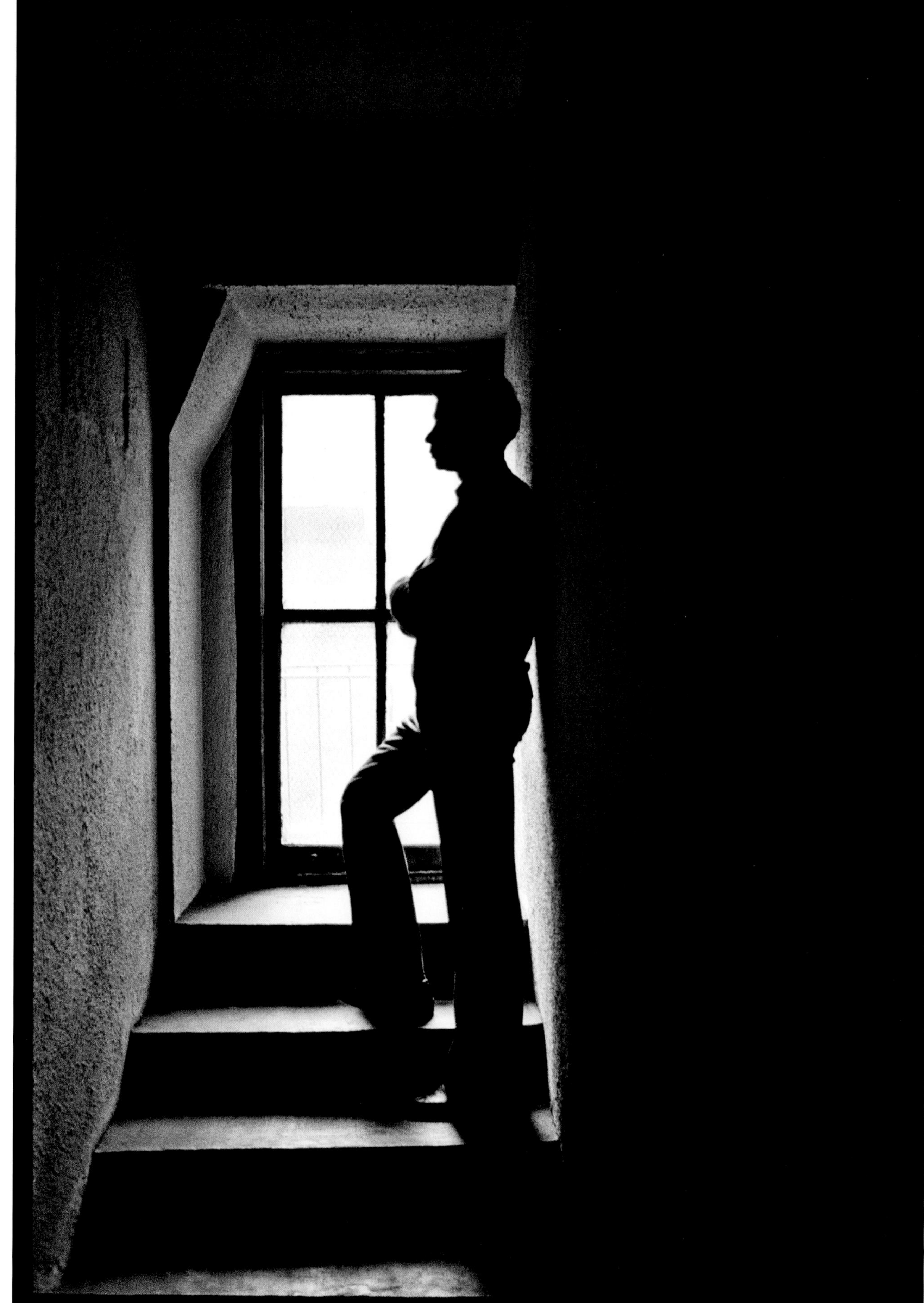

ABDULLAH IBRAHIM, 1981;
OPPOSITE:
DON CHERRY, 1982

36

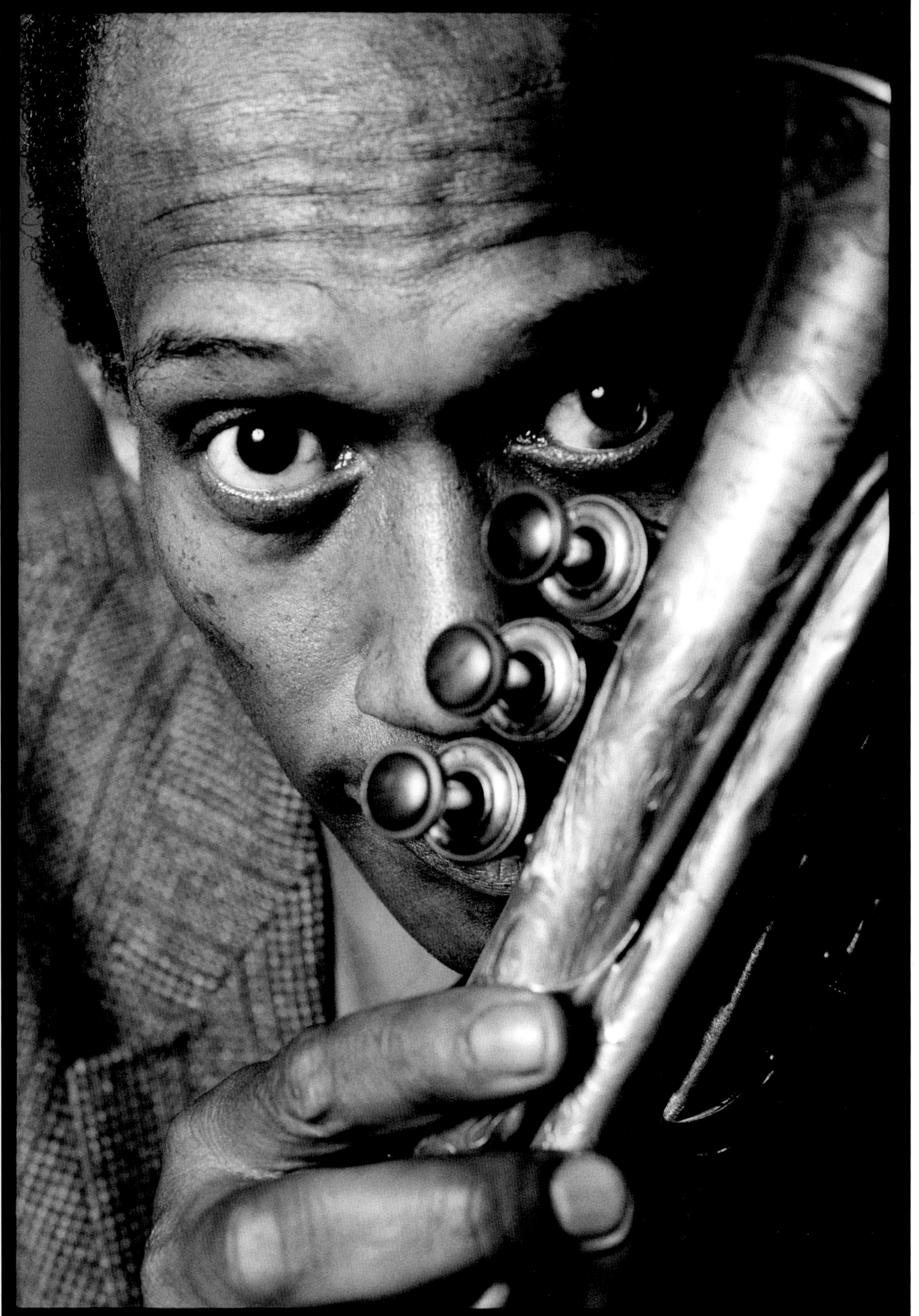

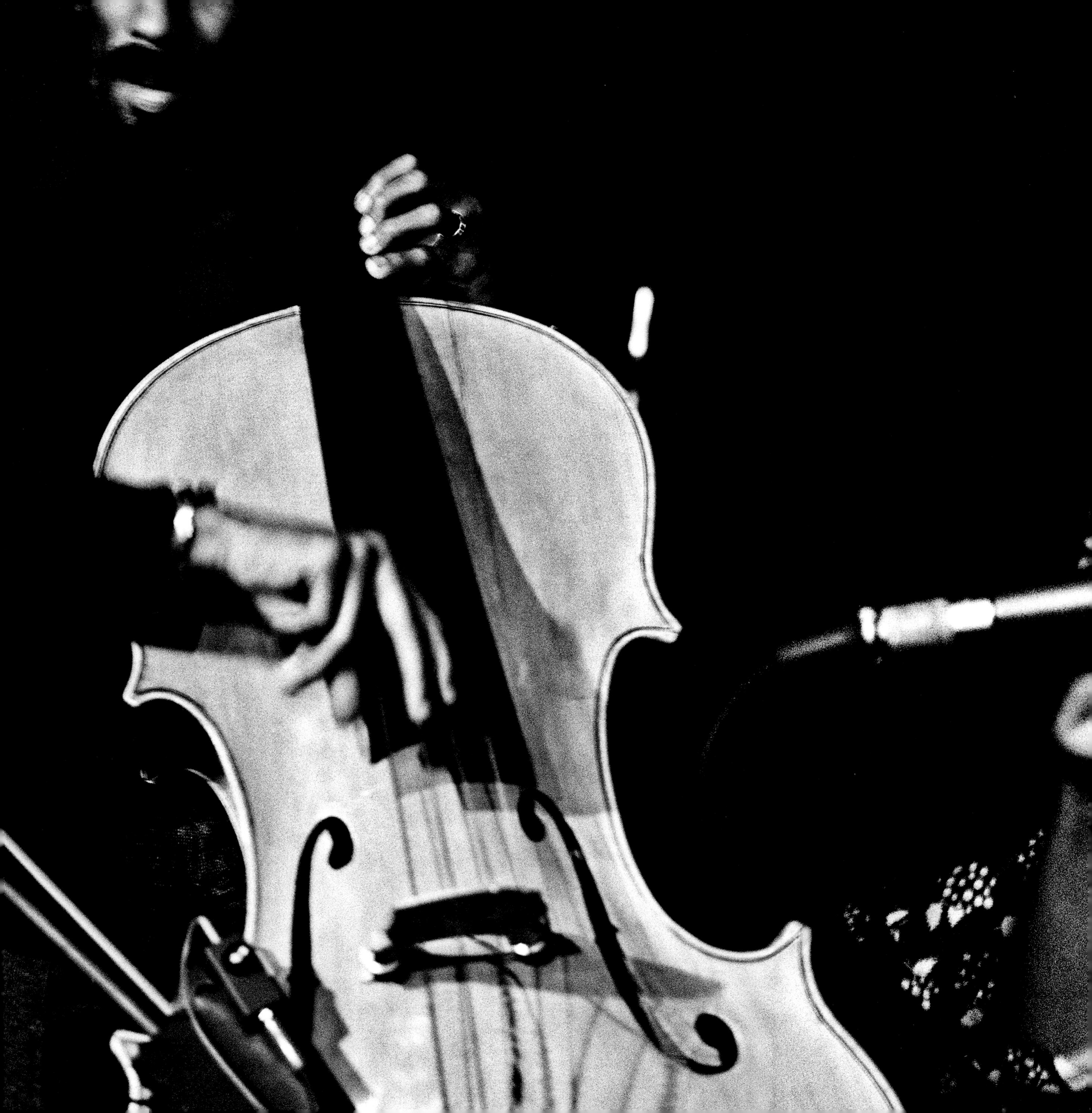

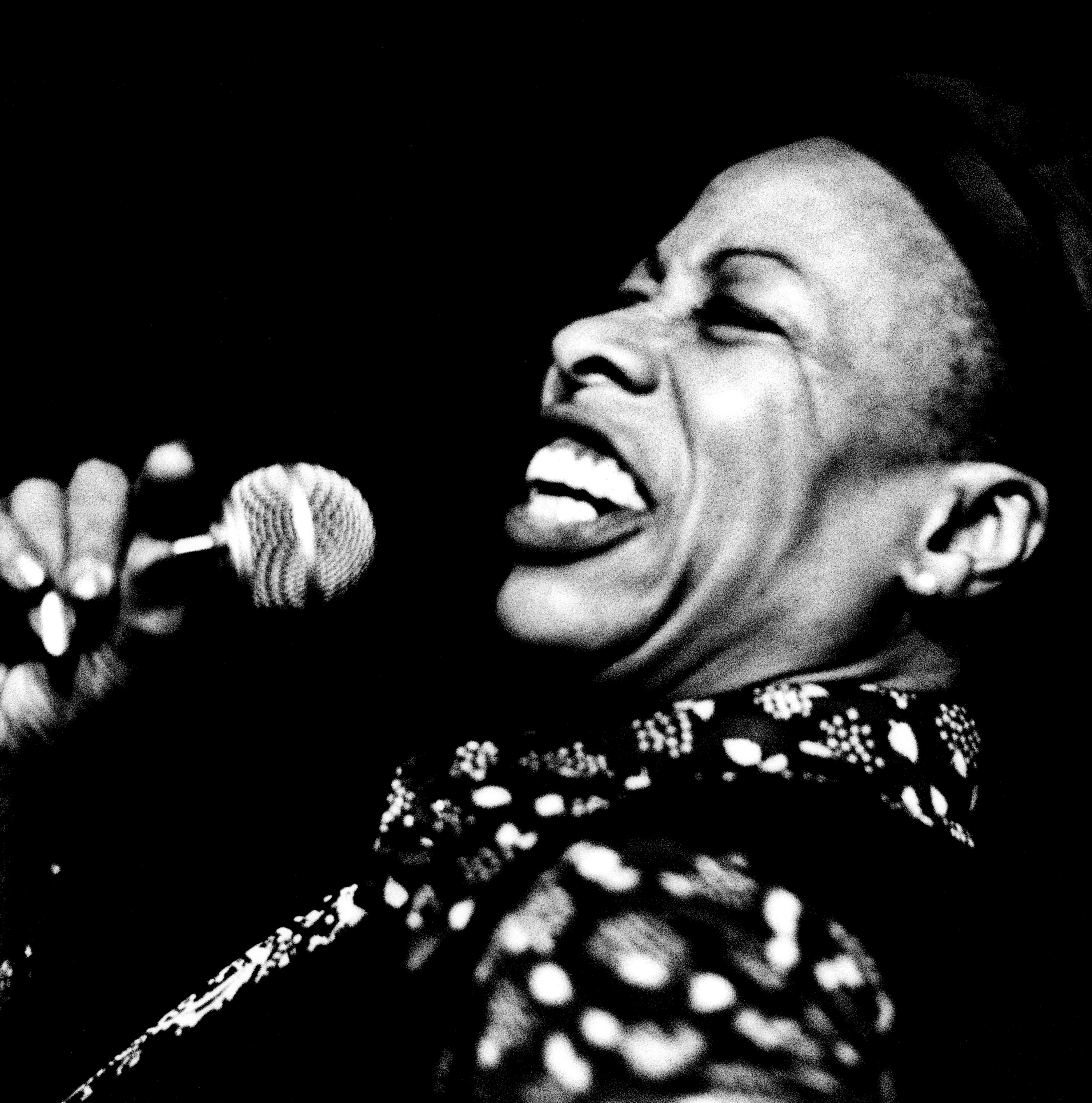

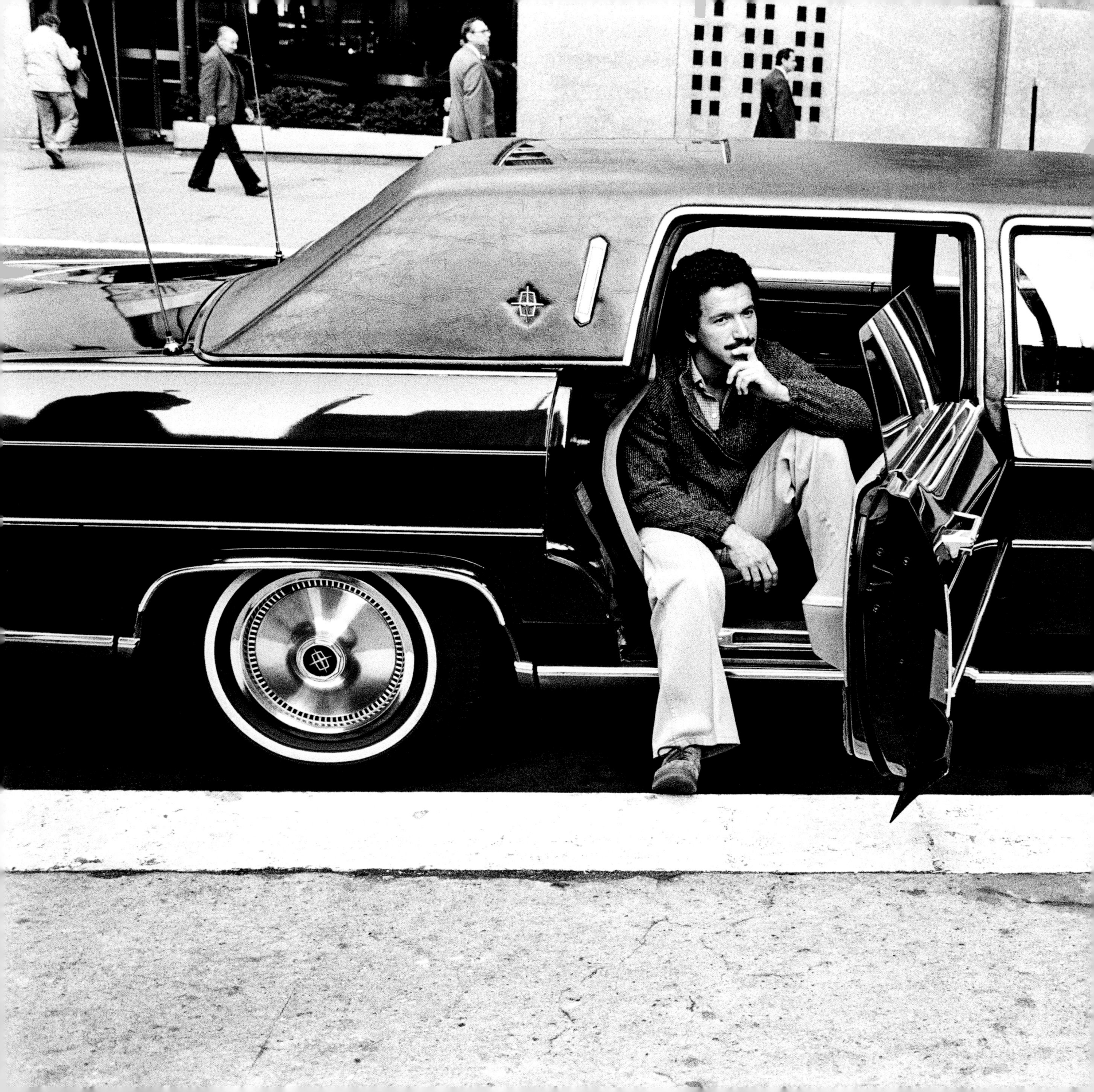

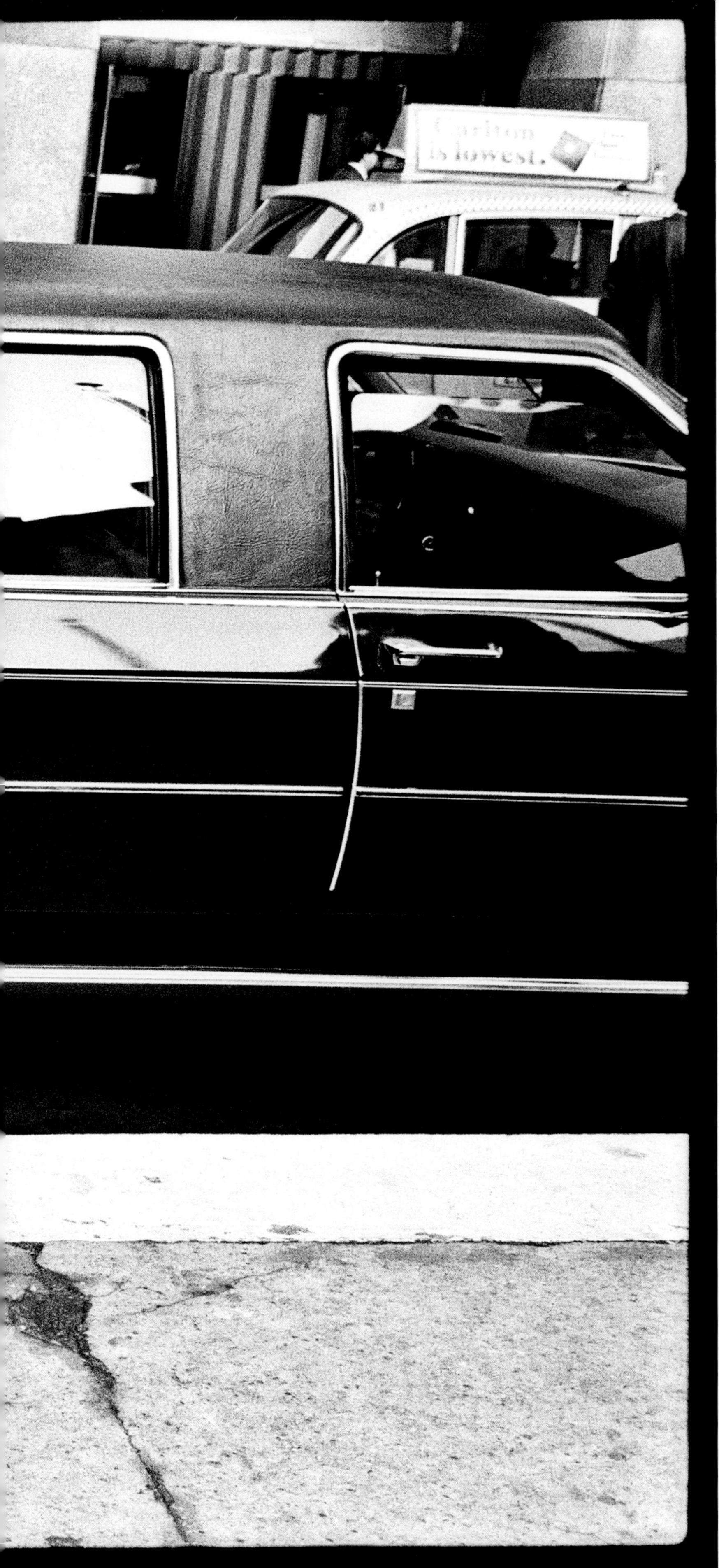

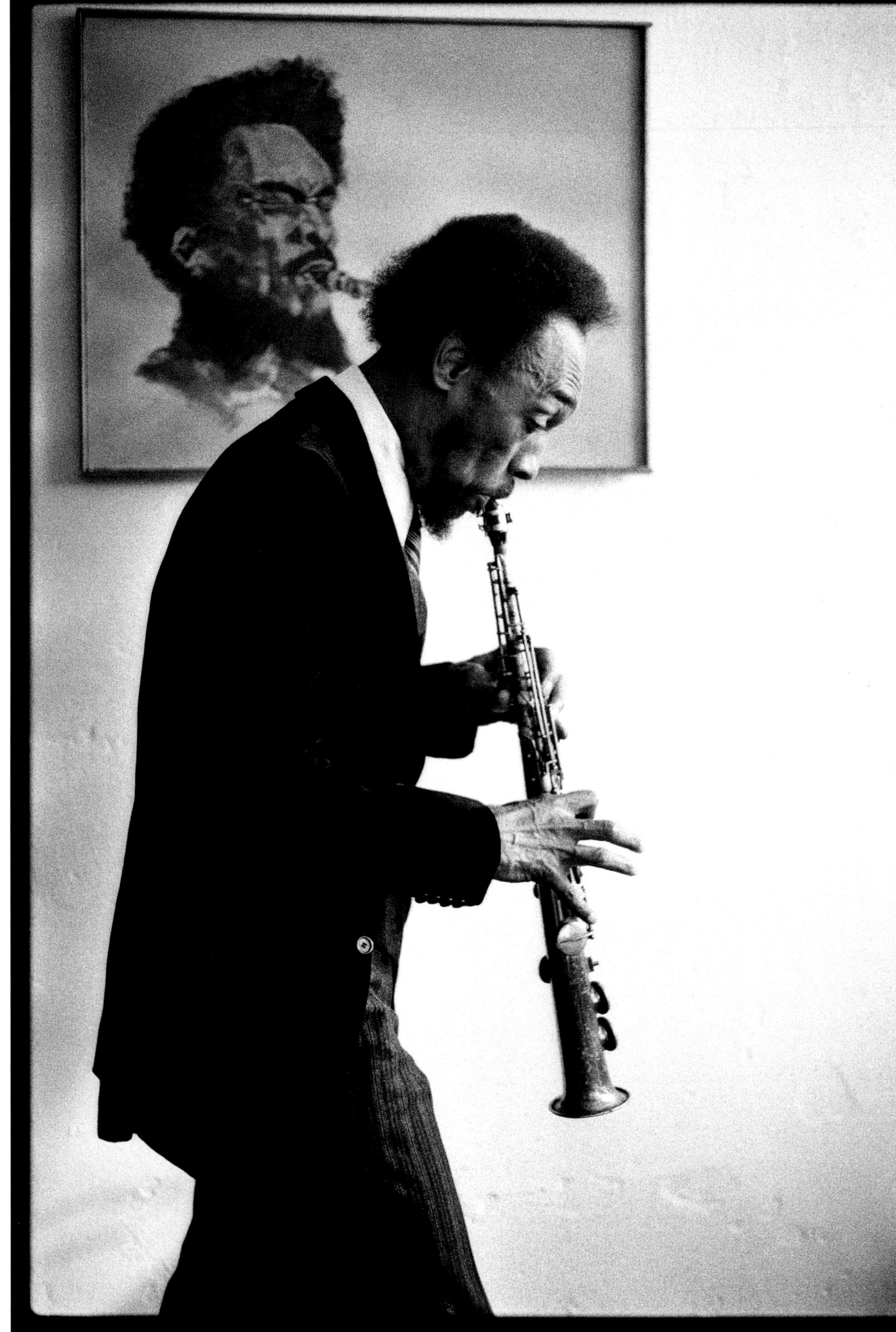

SAM RIVERS, 1980;
OPPOSITE: MAL WALDRON, 1982

42

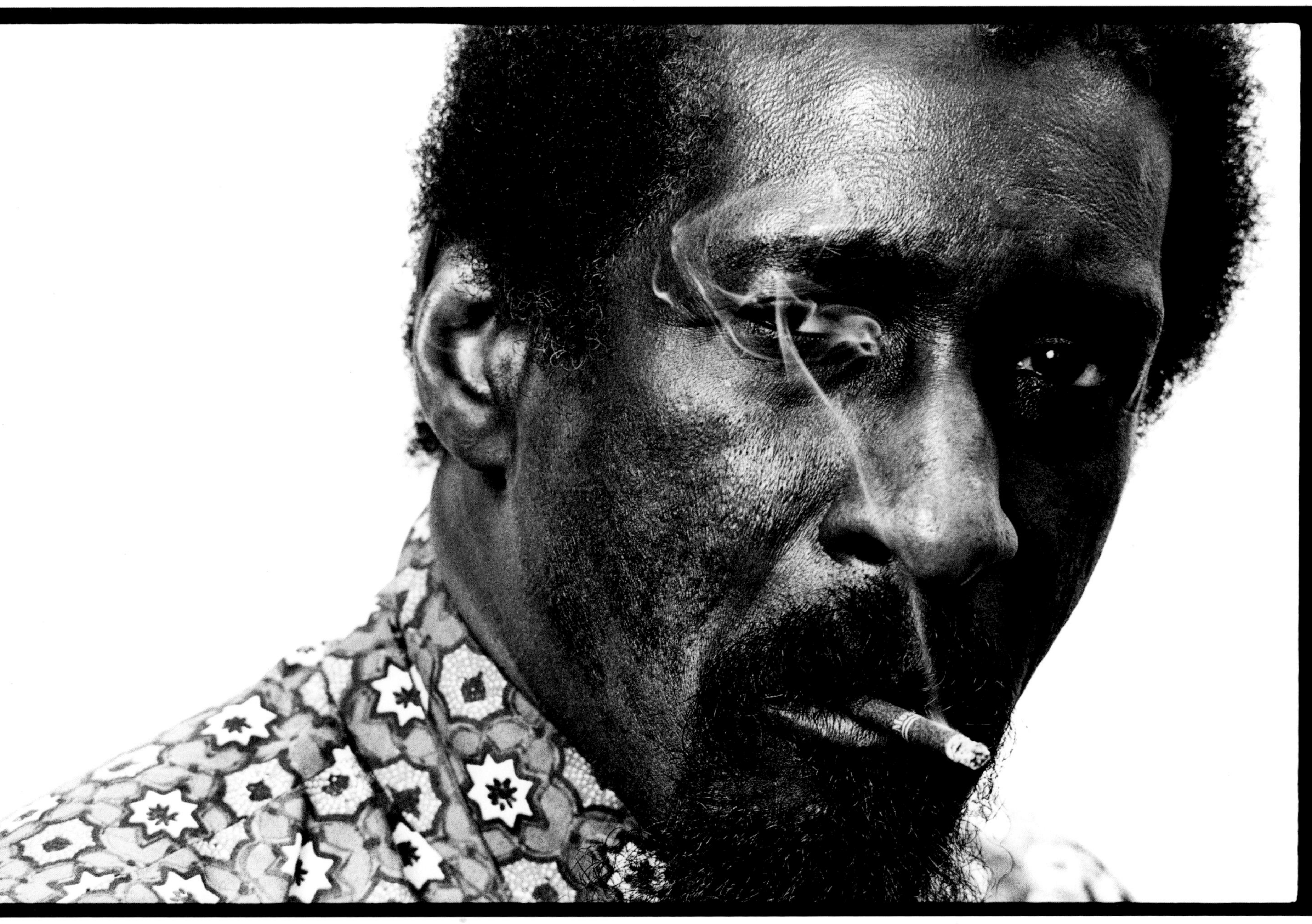

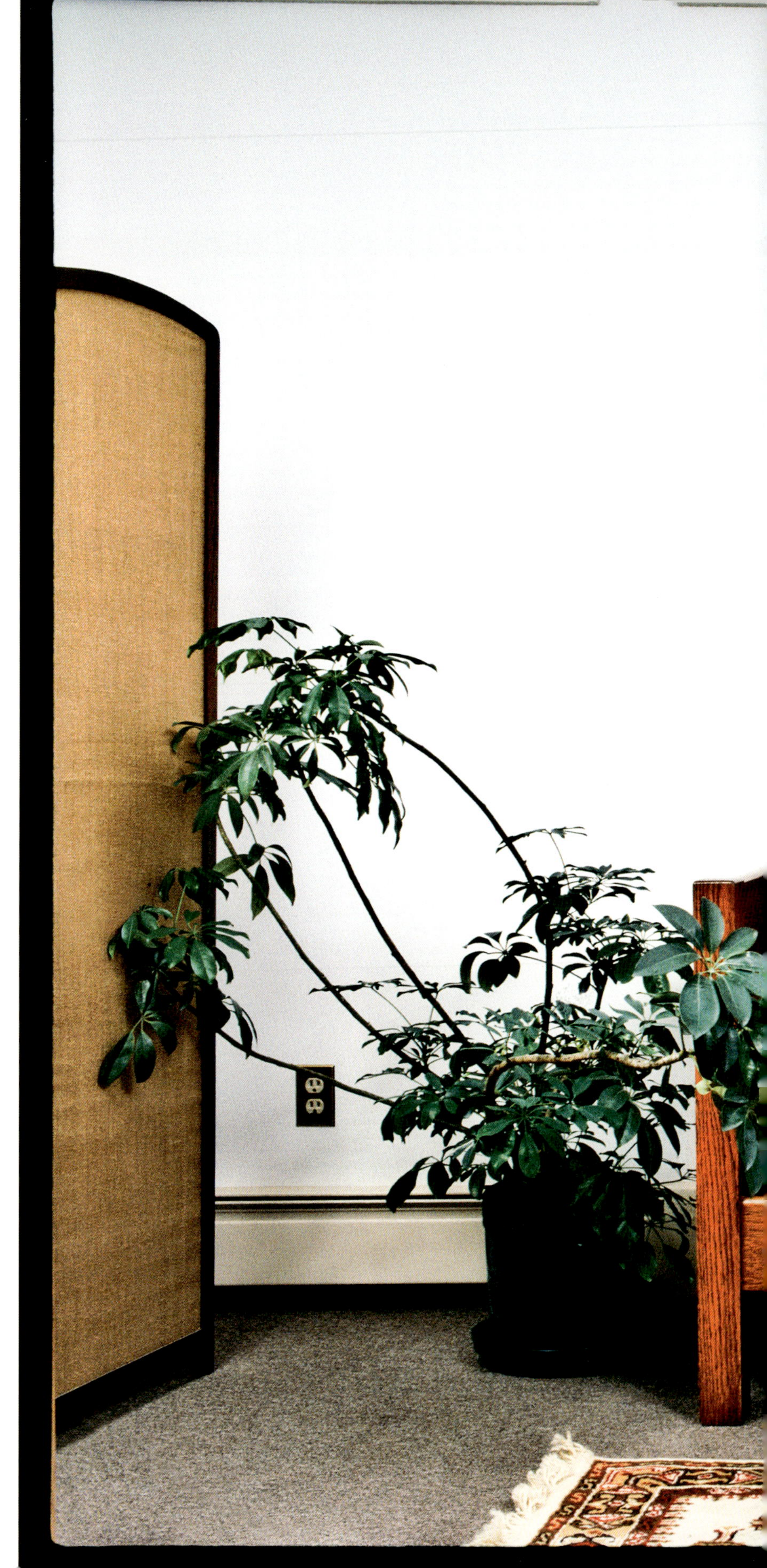

44

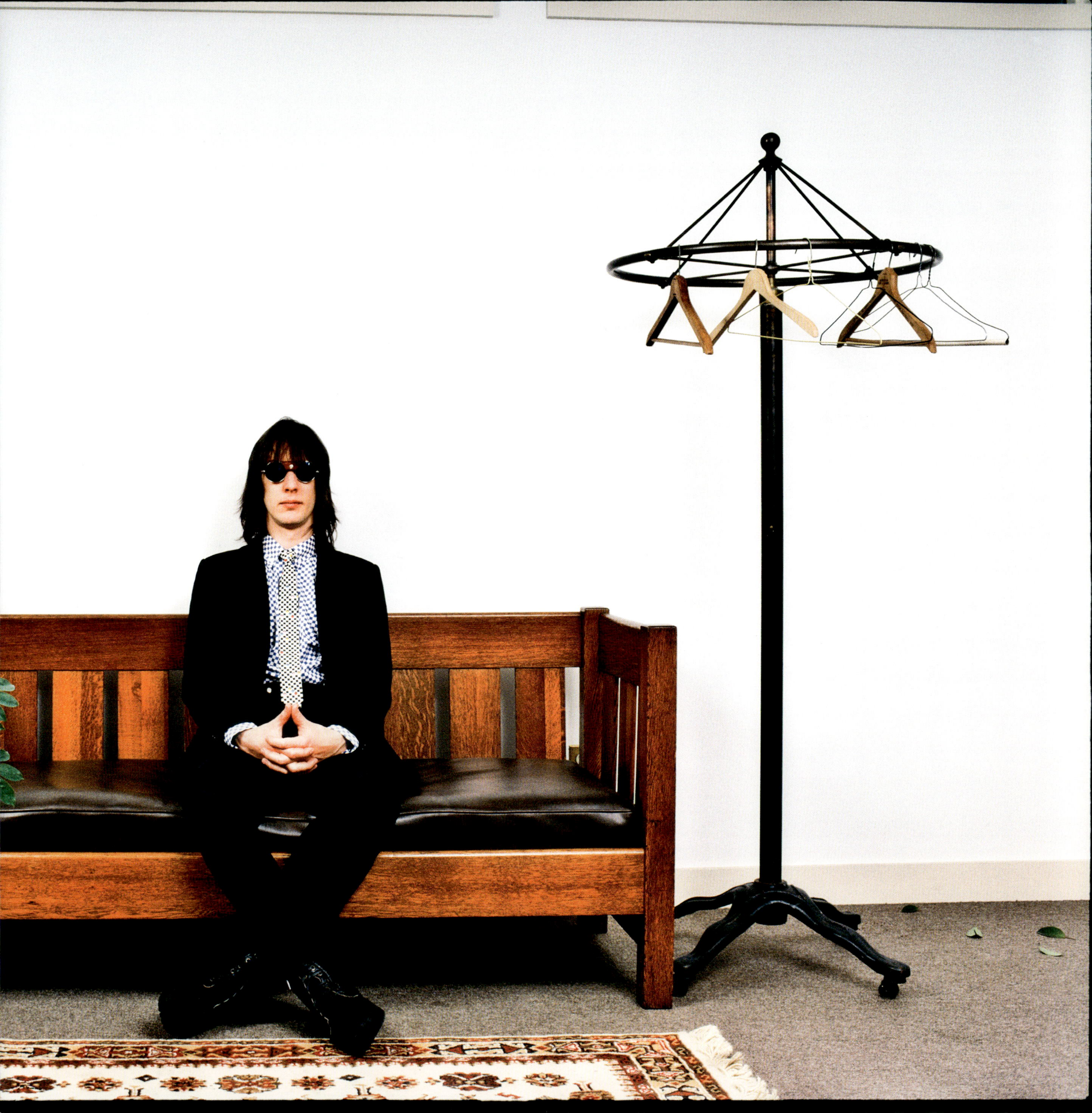

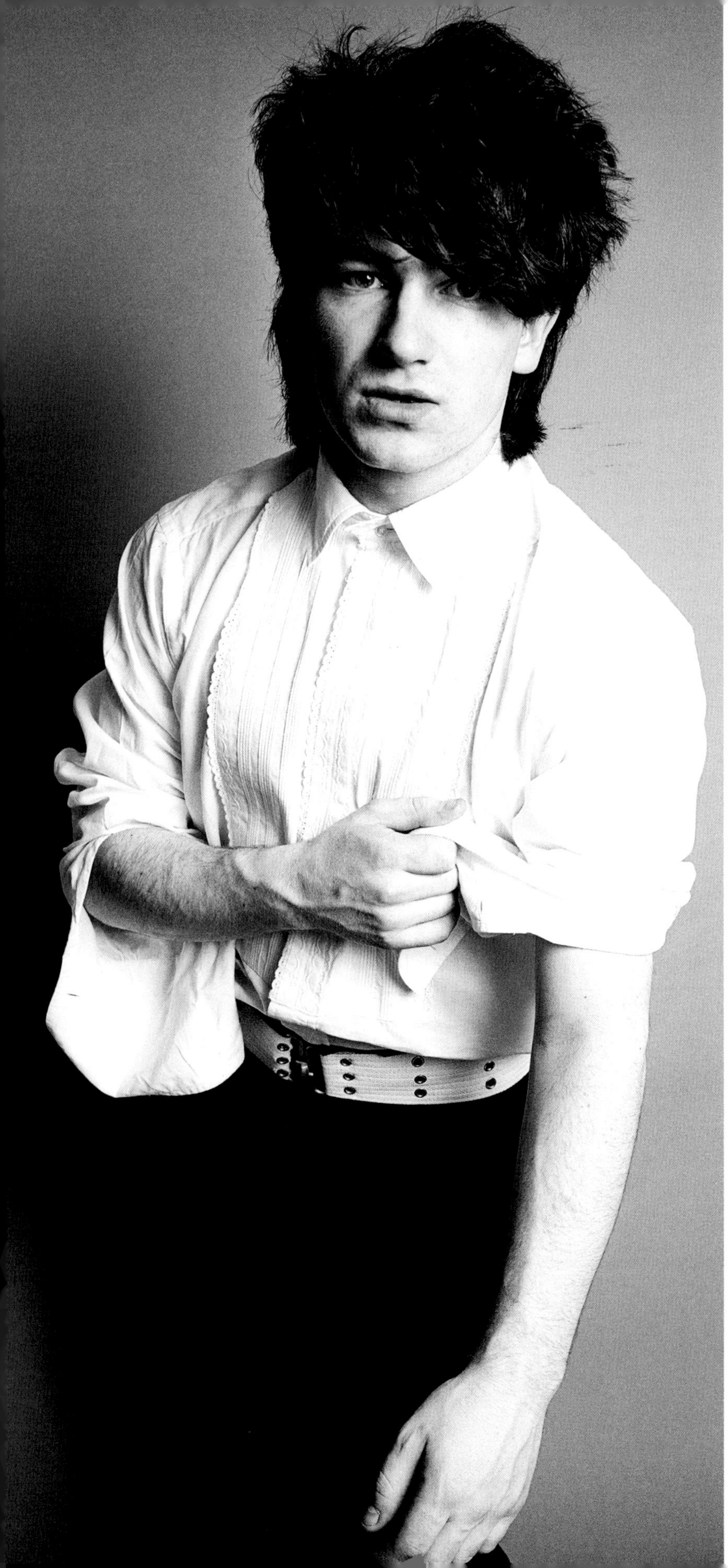

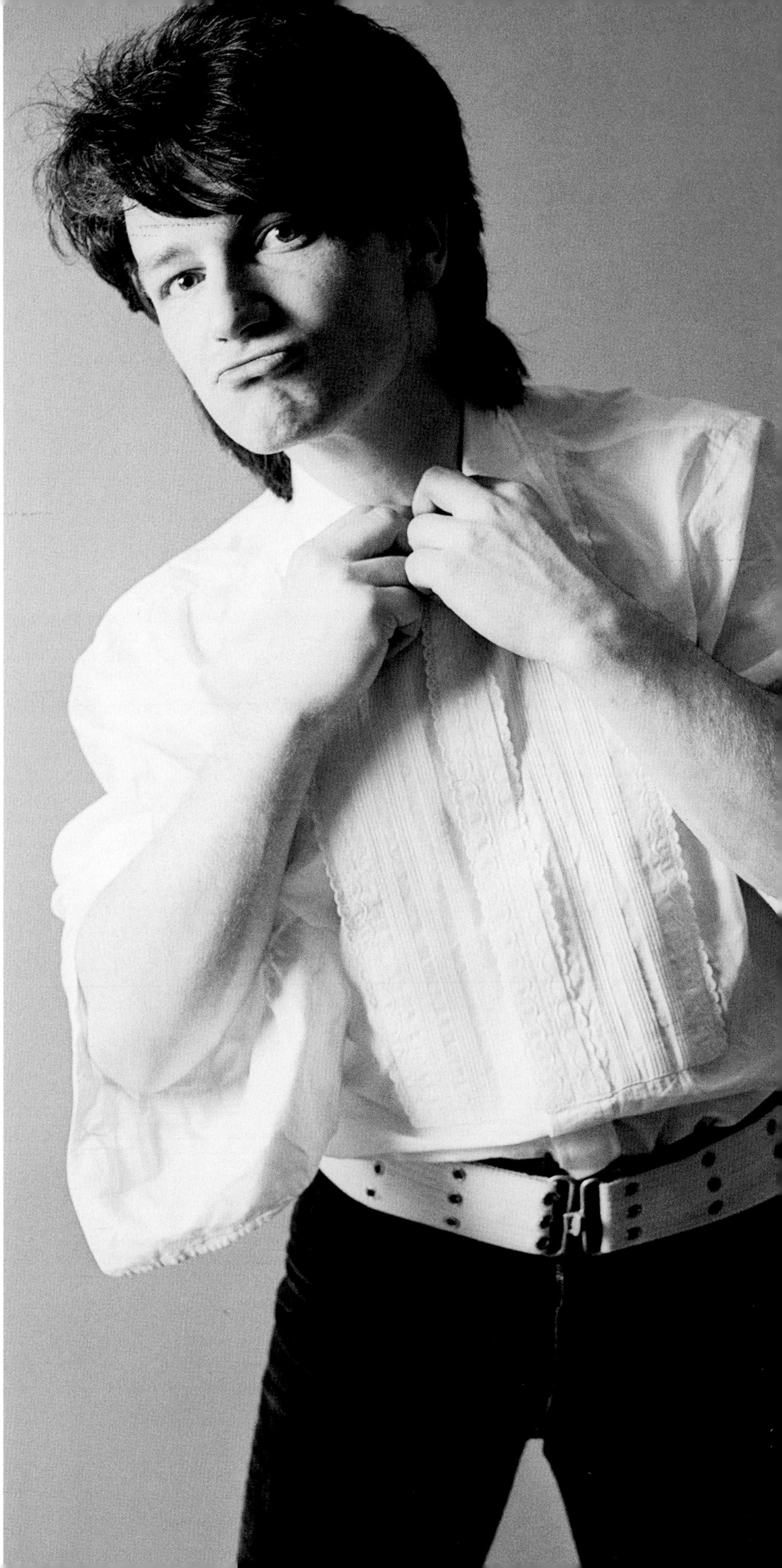

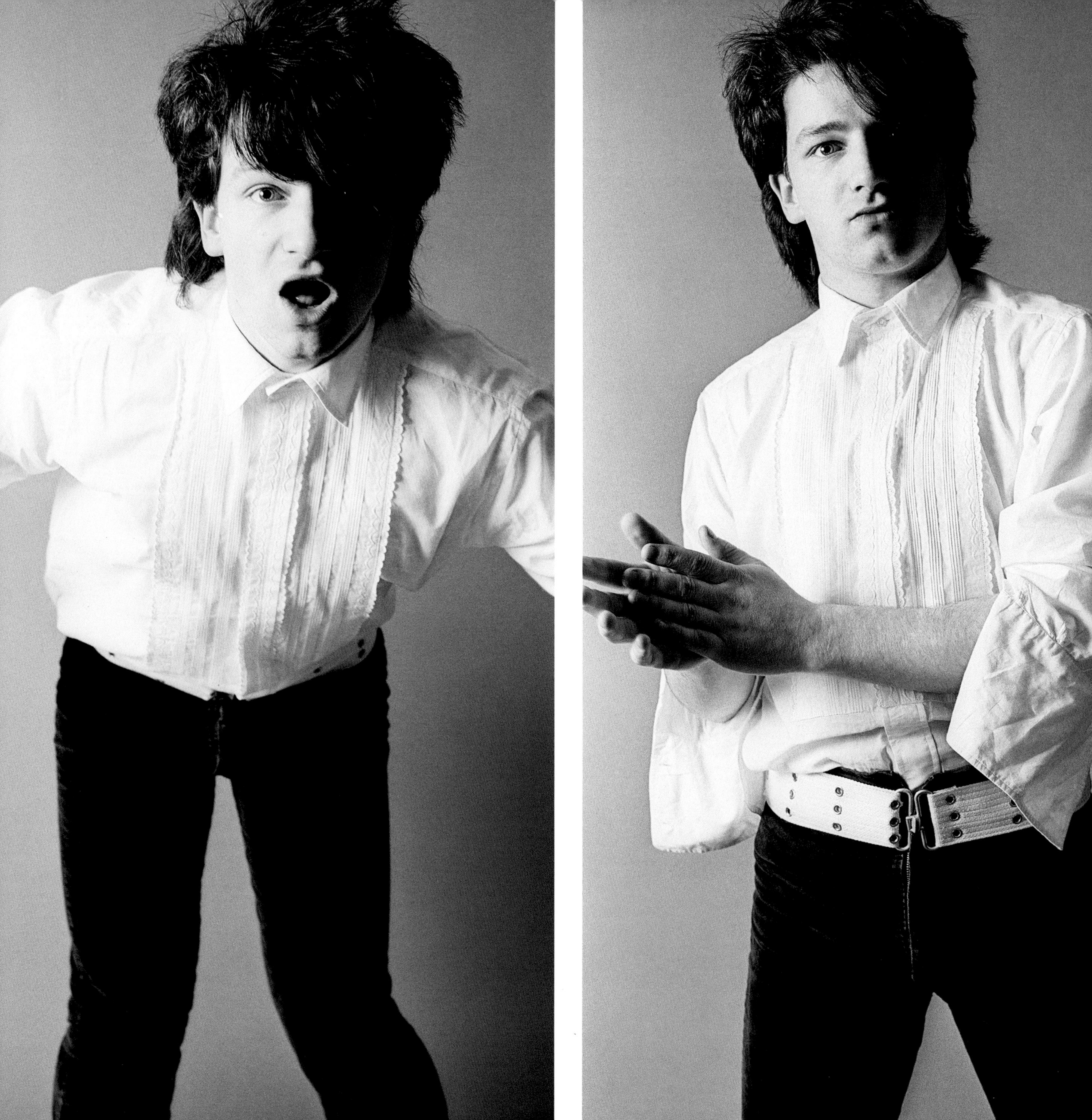

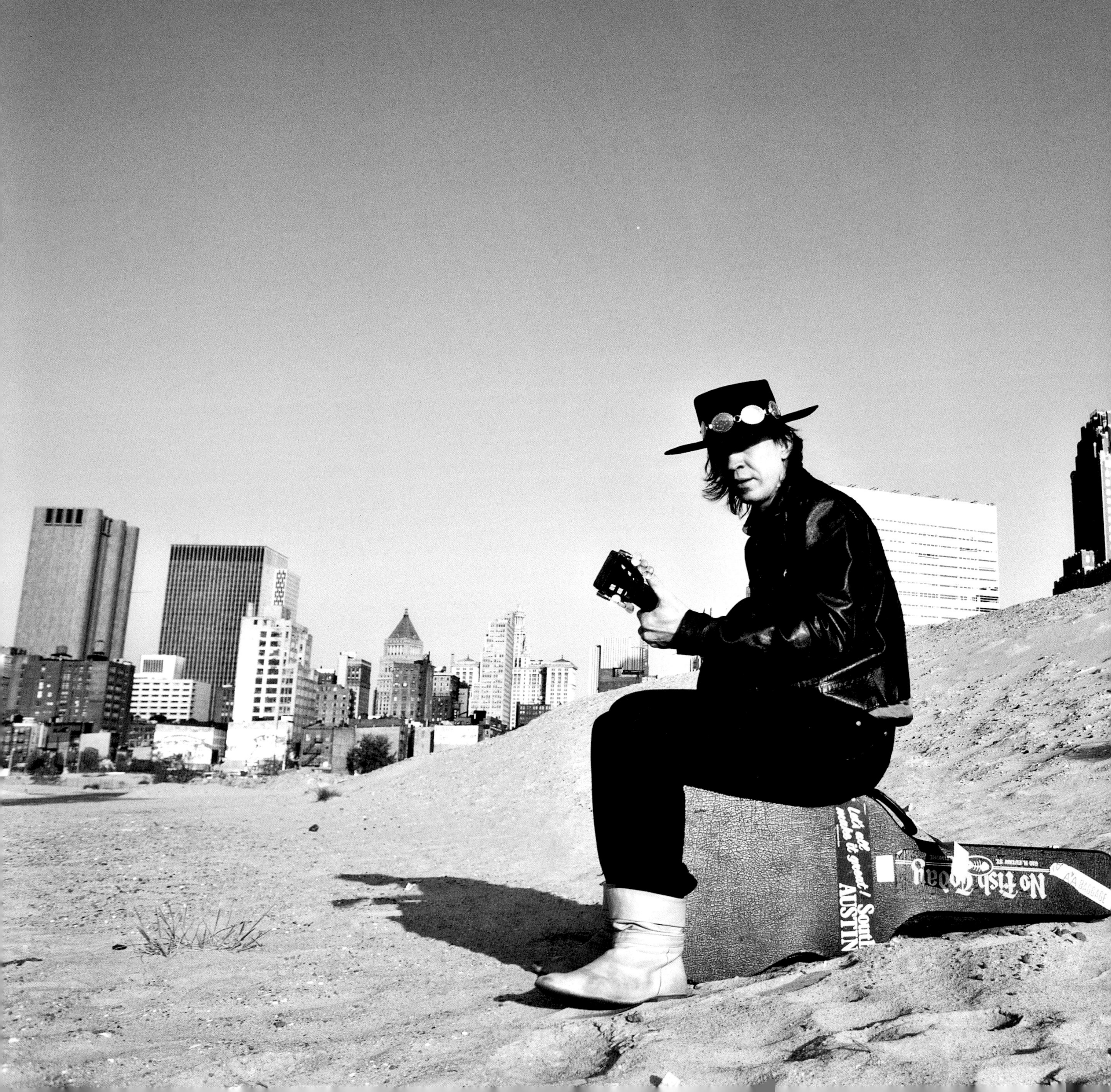
No fish today
Santi
AUSTIN

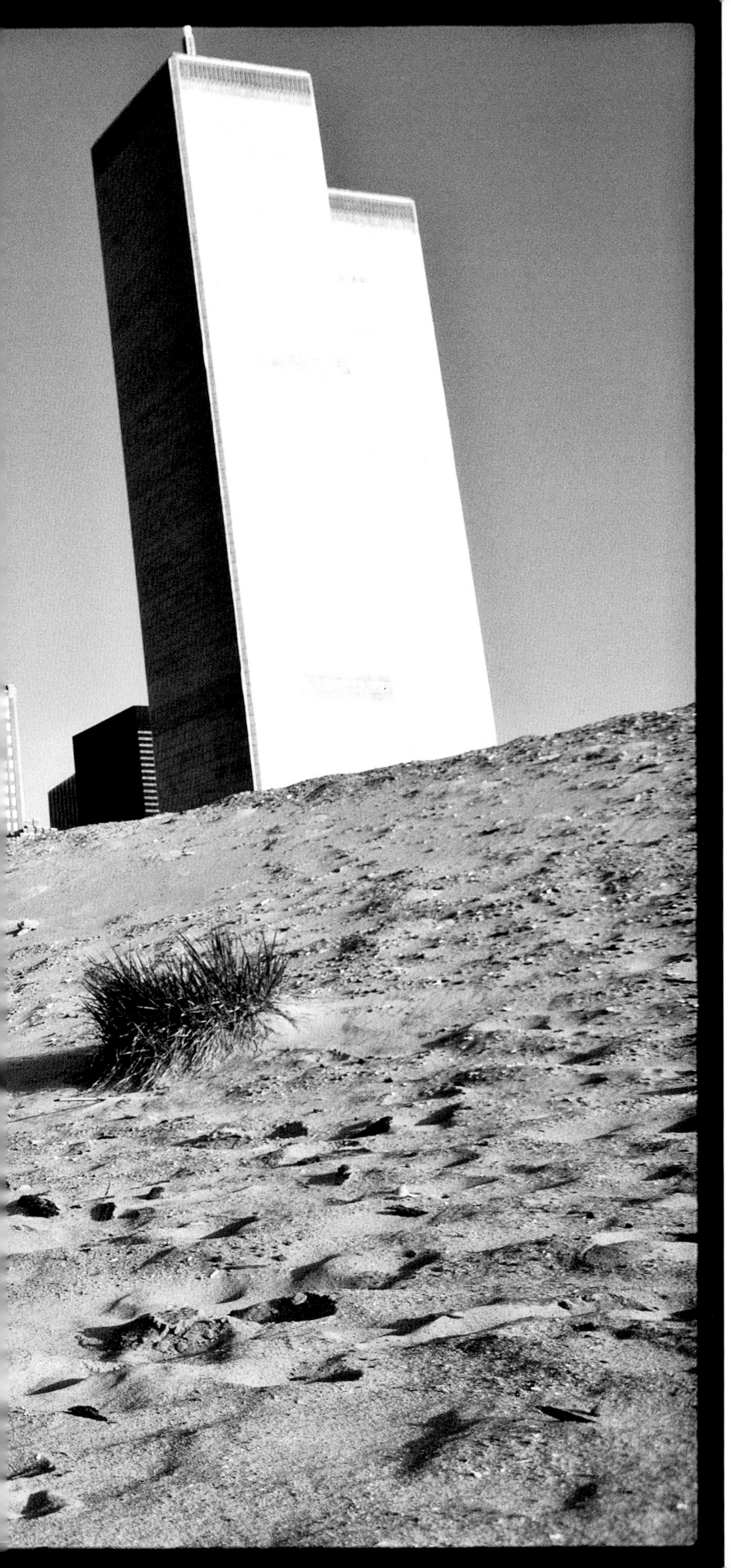

THIS SPREAD: STEVIE RAY VAUGHAN, 1983
PAGE 50: GRACE JONES MASKS CREATED BY JEAN-PAUL GOUDE, 1983;
PAGE 51: PETER GABRIEL, 1983

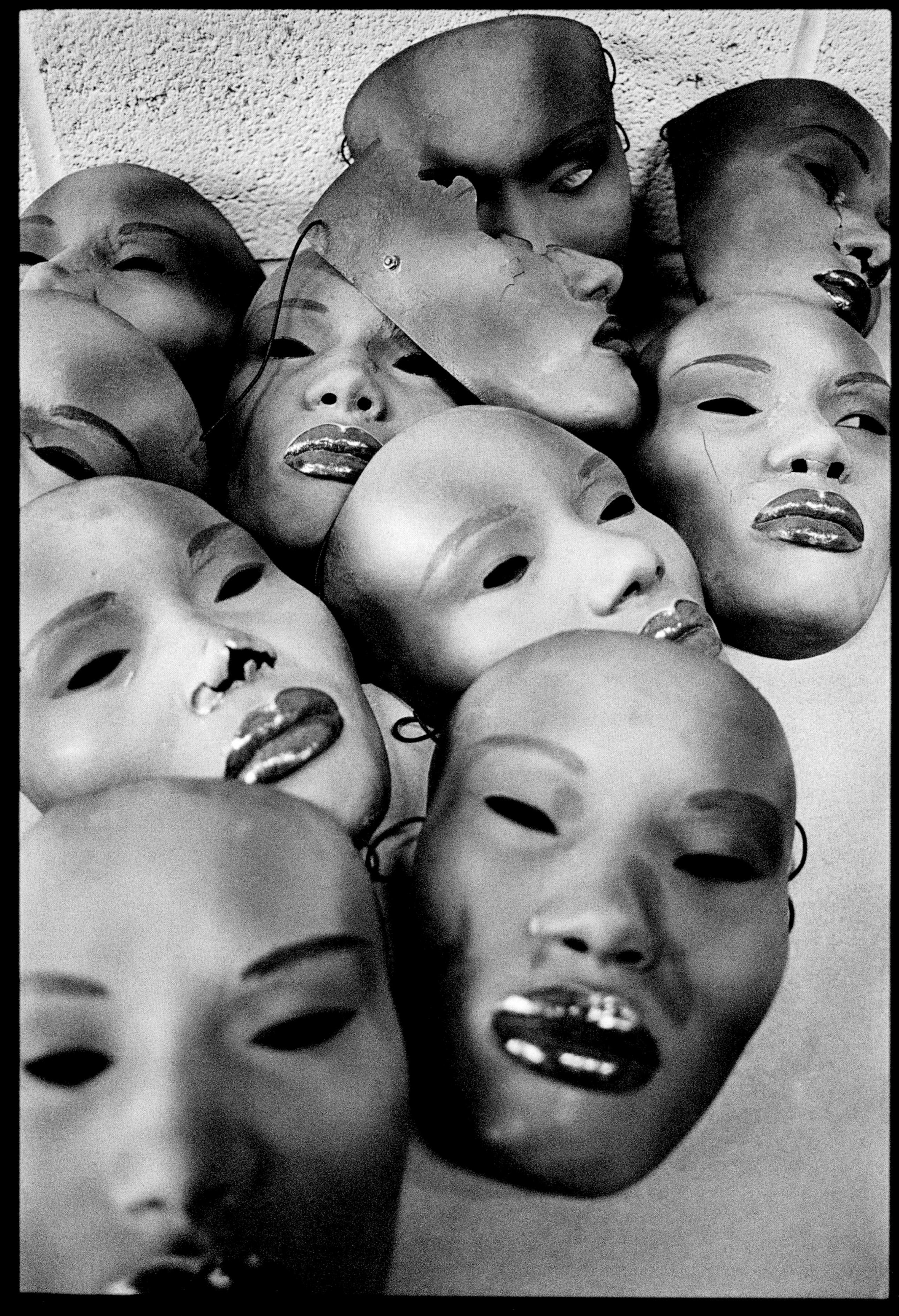

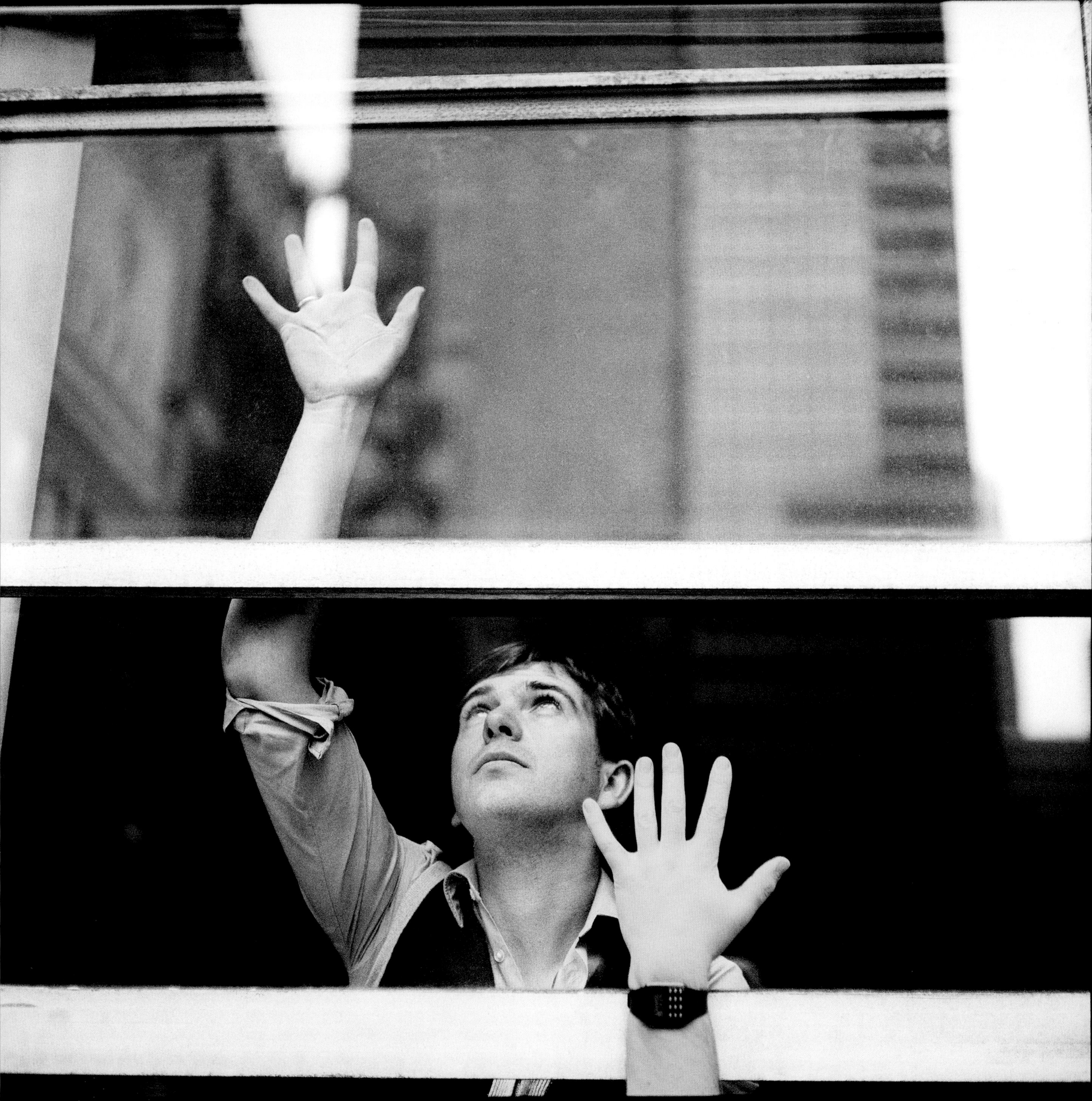

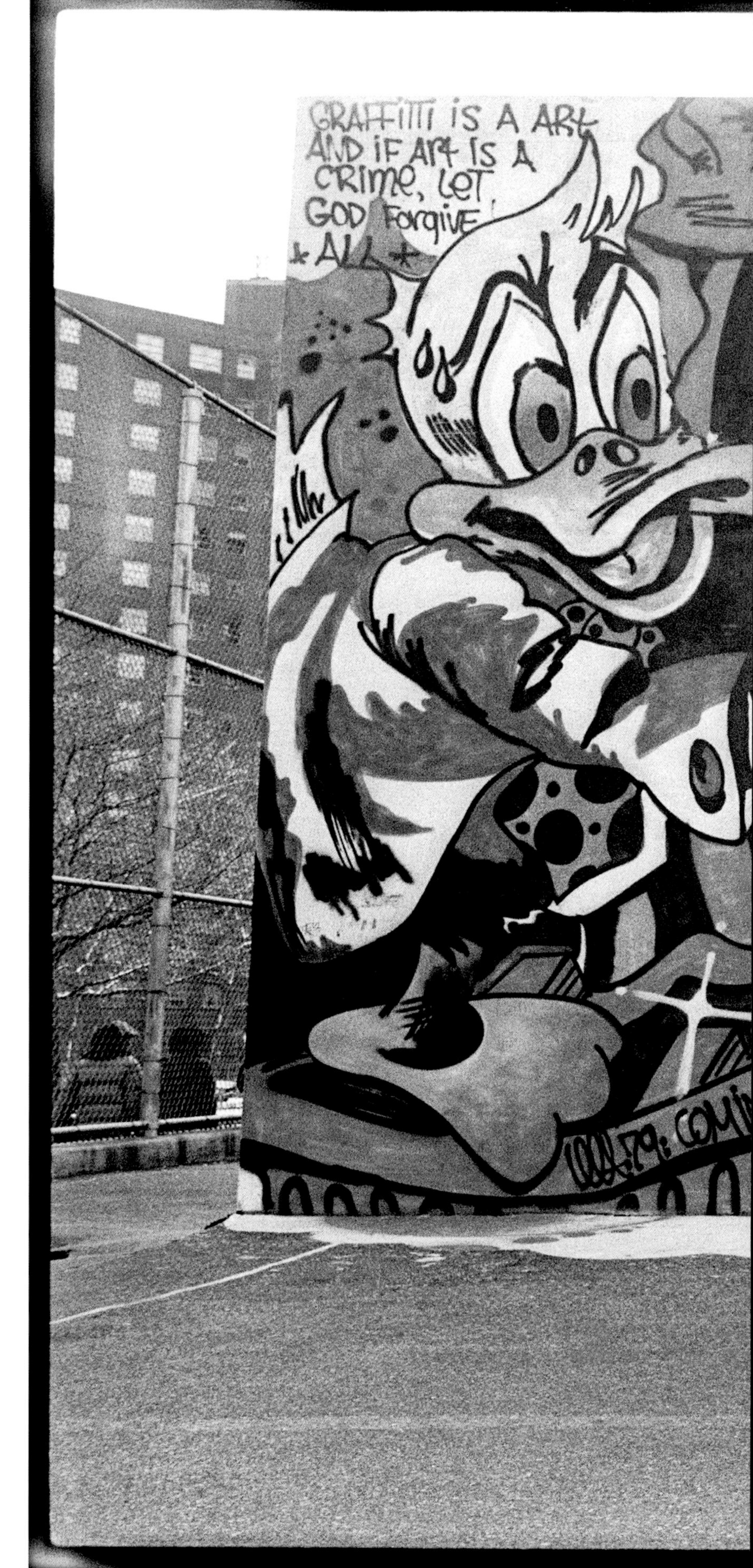

FAB 5 FREDDY, 1979 (MURAL BY LEE QUINONES)

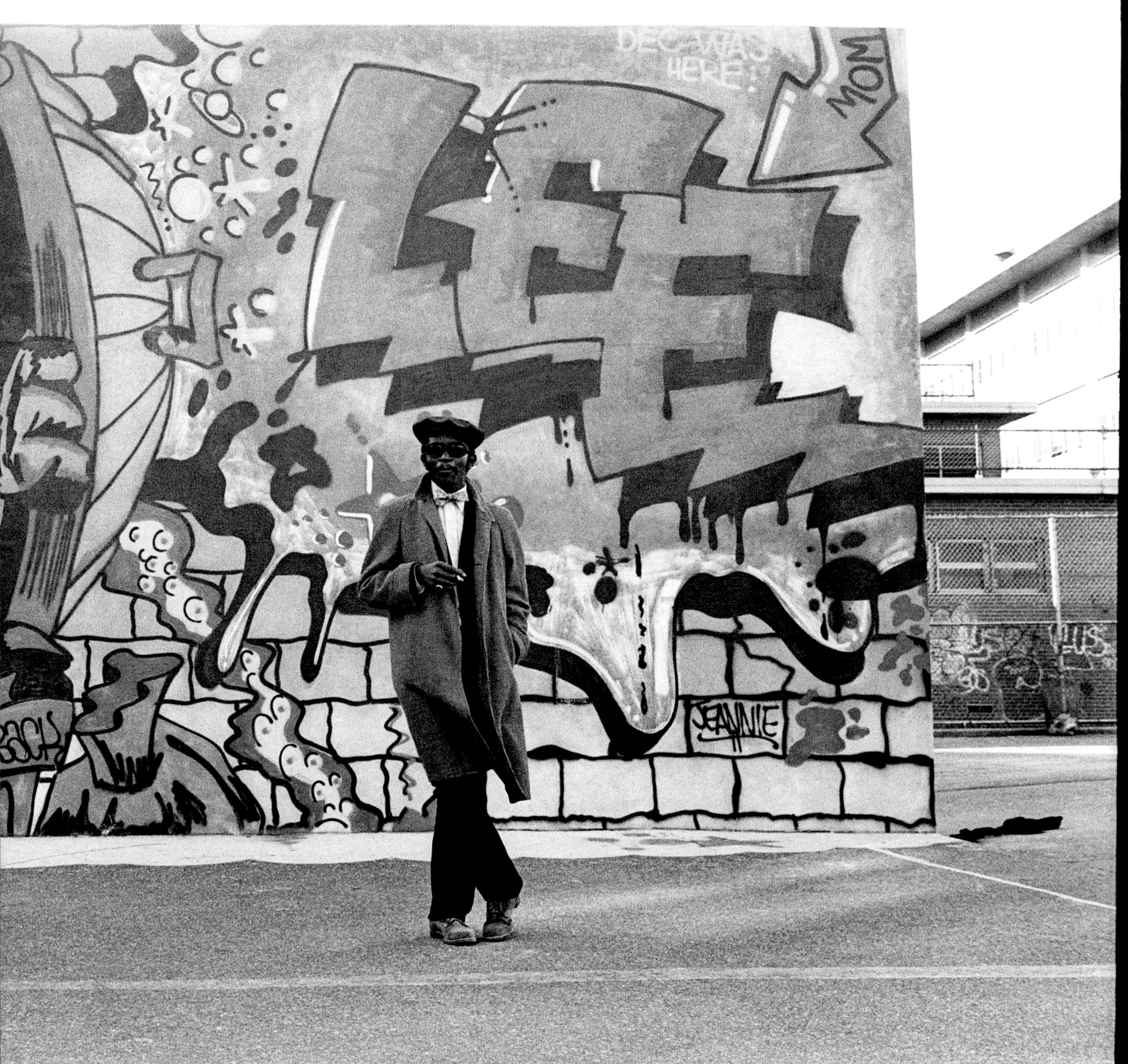

DEC WAS HERE!
MOM
JEANNIE

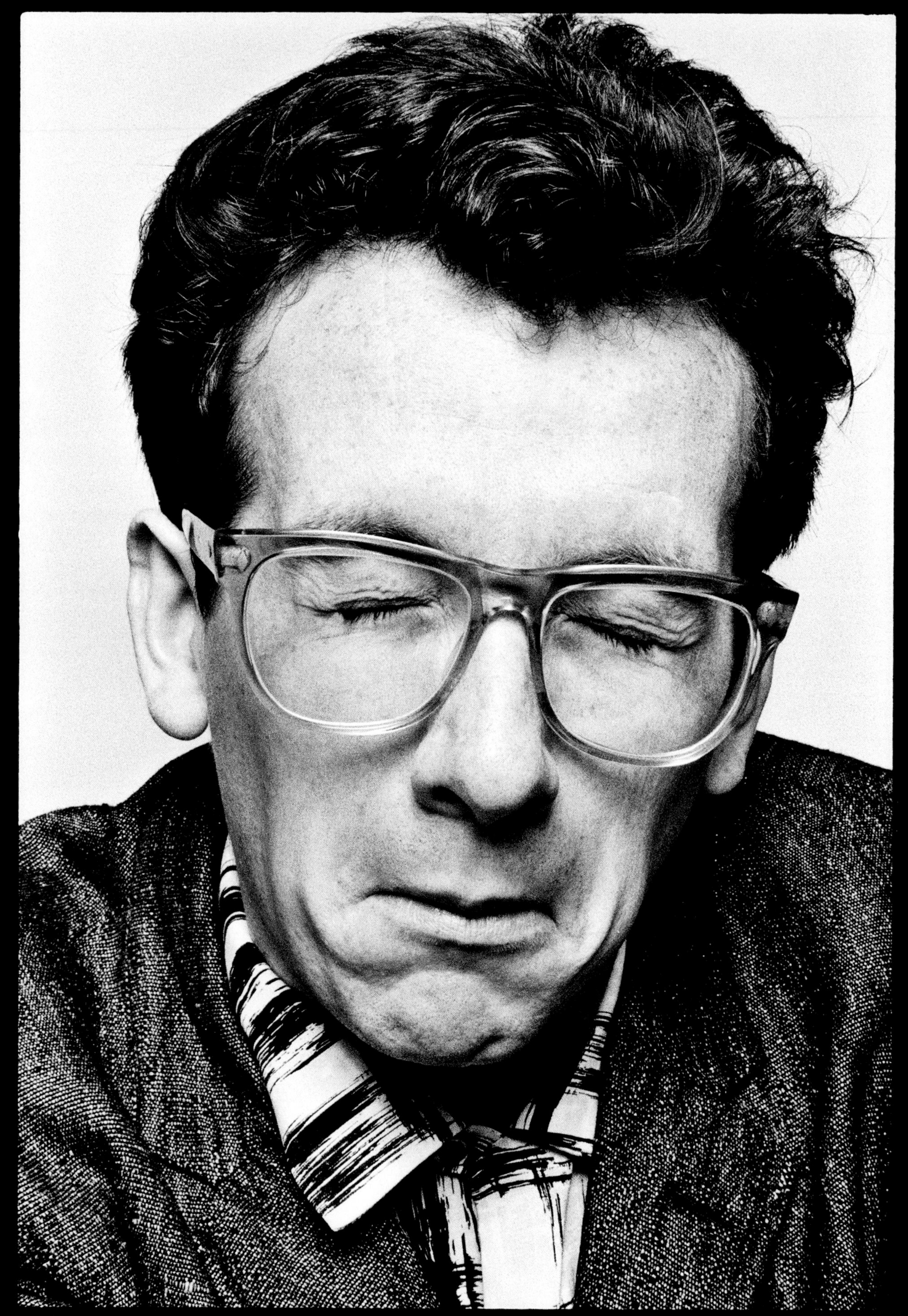

ELVIS COSTELLO, 1982;
OPPOSITE:
BOY GEORGE, 1983

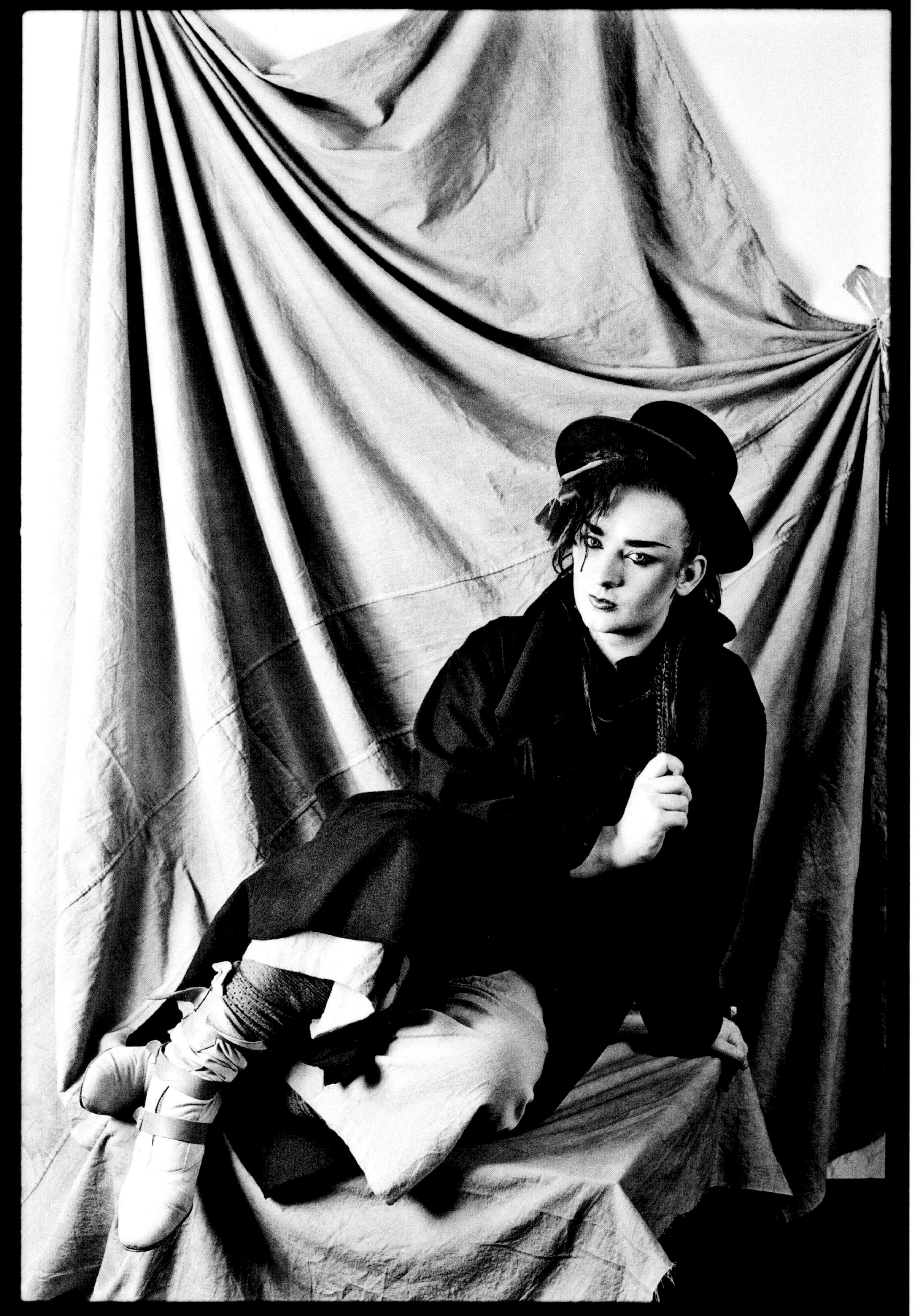

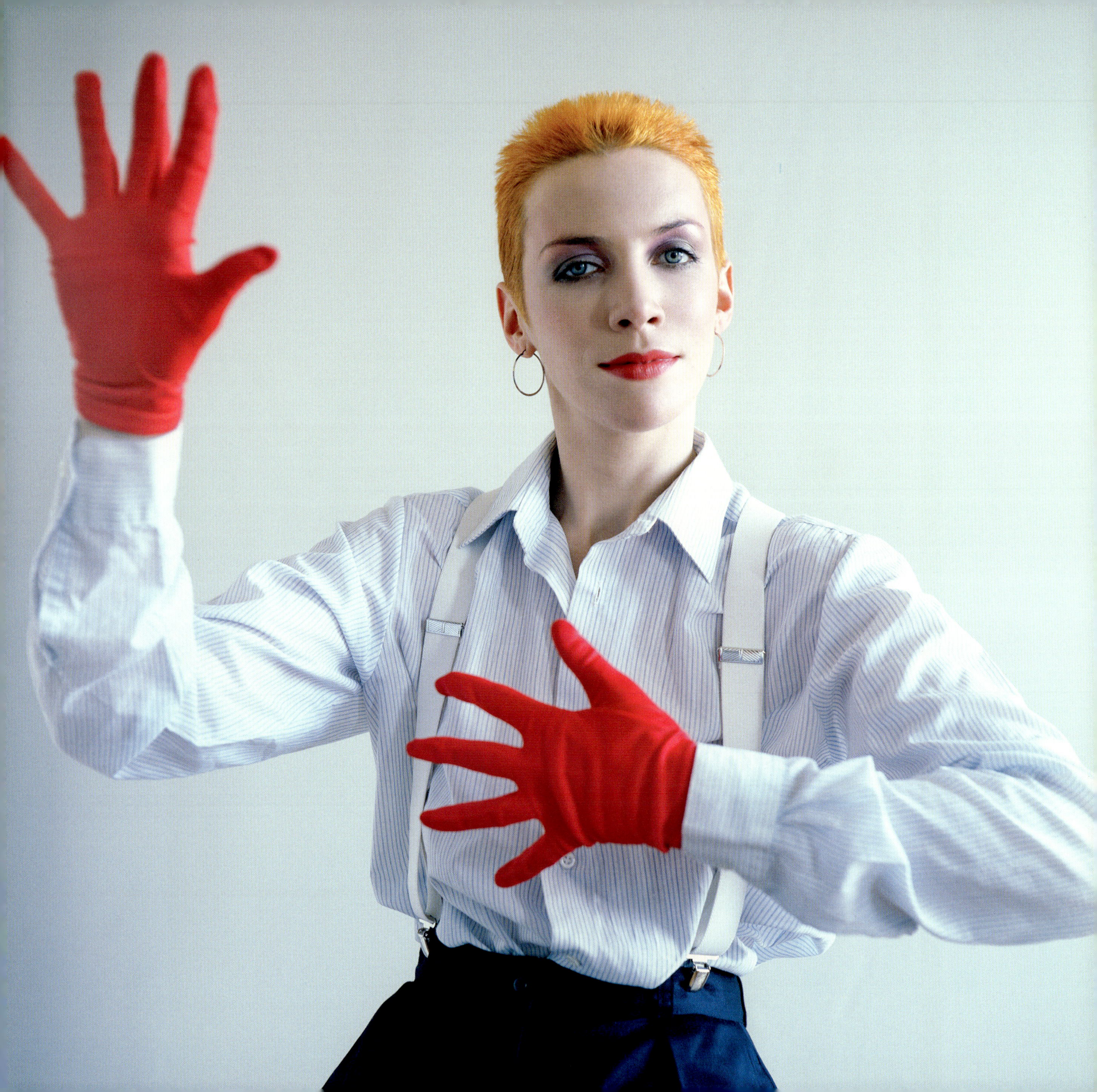

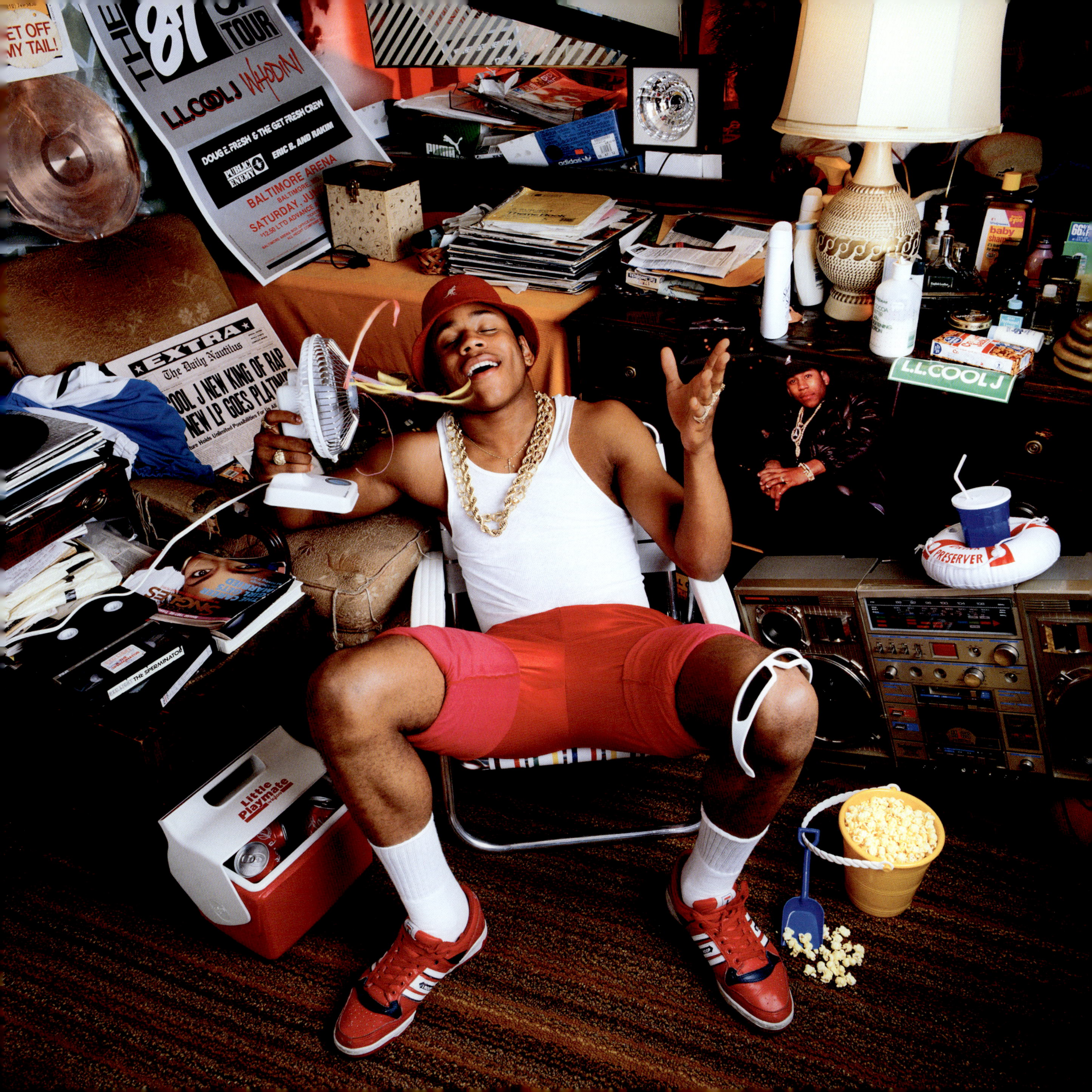
GET OFF MY TAIL!
THE '87 TOUR
L.L. COOL J
WHODINI
DOUG E. FRESH & THE GET FRESH CREW
PUBLIC ENEMY
ERIC B. AND RAKIM
BALTIMORE ARENA
BALTIMORE
SATURDAY, JU
$12.50 LTD ADVANCE
EXTRA
The Daily Nautilus
COOL J NEW KING OF RAP
NEW LP GOES PLATINUM
Future Holds Unlimited Possibilities For Us All
PUMA
adidas
baby sham
L.L. COOL J
PRESERVER
Little Playmate
THE SPERMINATOR

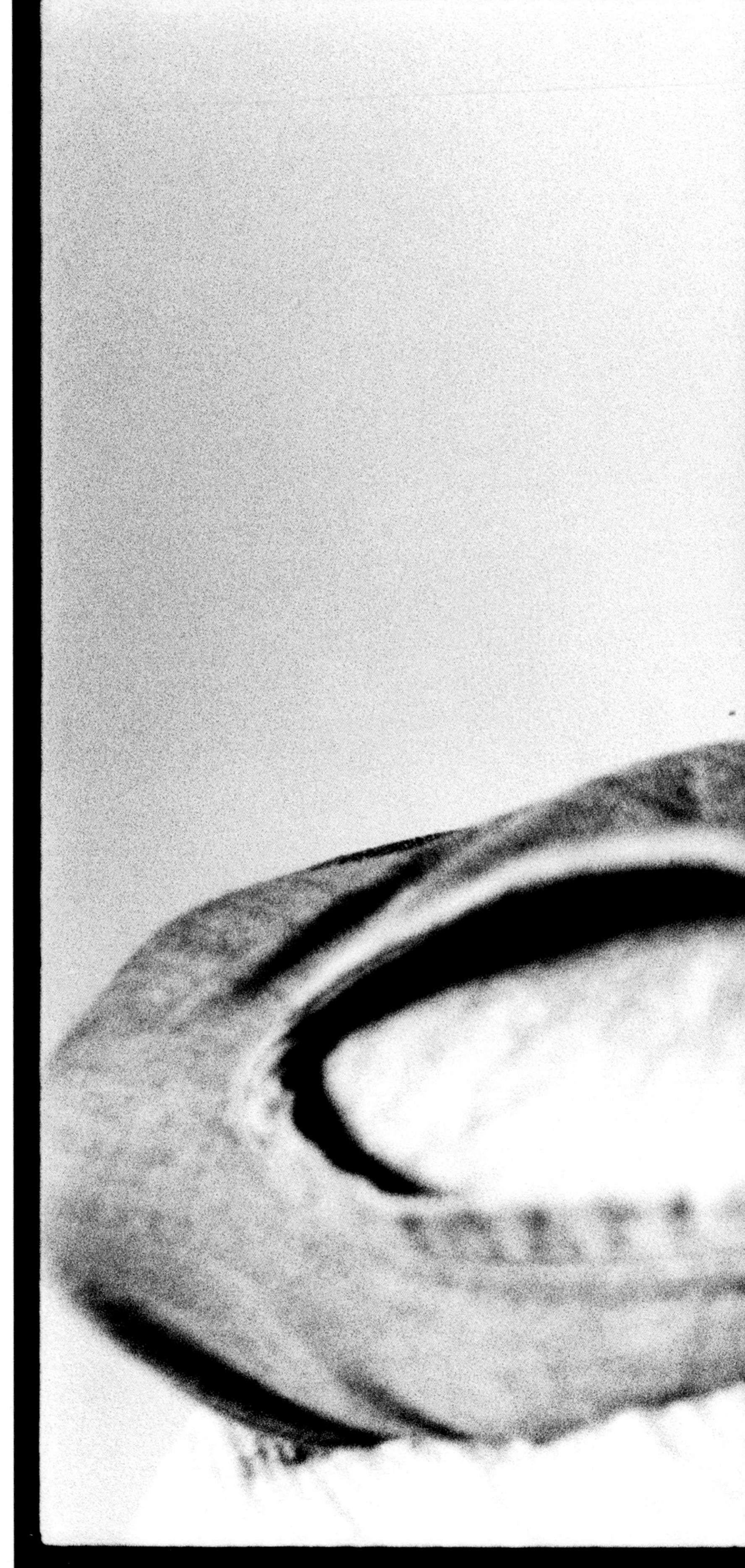

PAGE 56: ANNIE LENNOX, 1983; PAGE 57: L.L. COOL J, 1987
THIS SPREAD: PHILIP GLASS, 1982
PAGE 60: QUESTLOVE, 2013;
PAGE 61: LEONARD COHEN AND SUZANNE VEGA, 1989

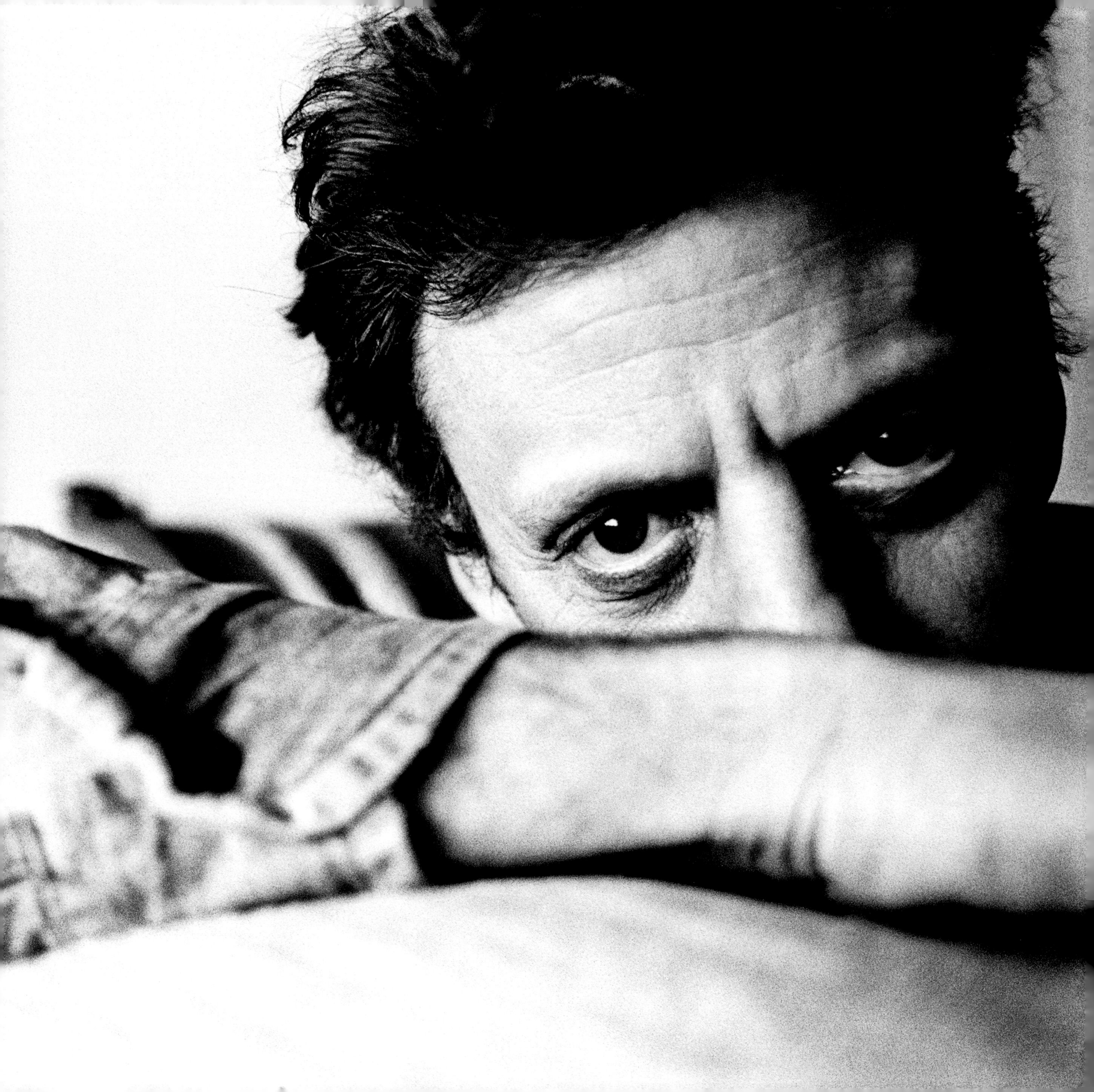

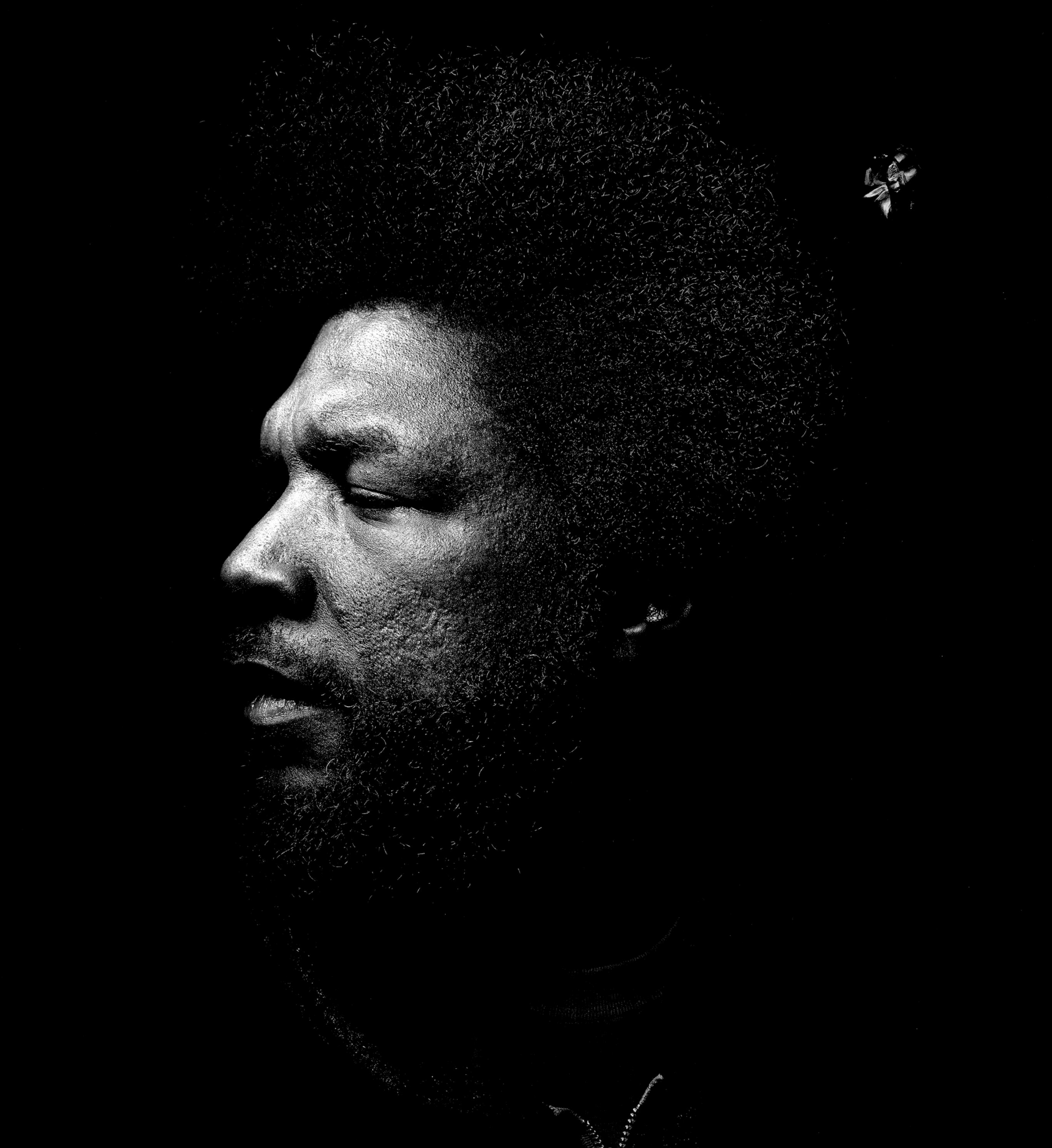

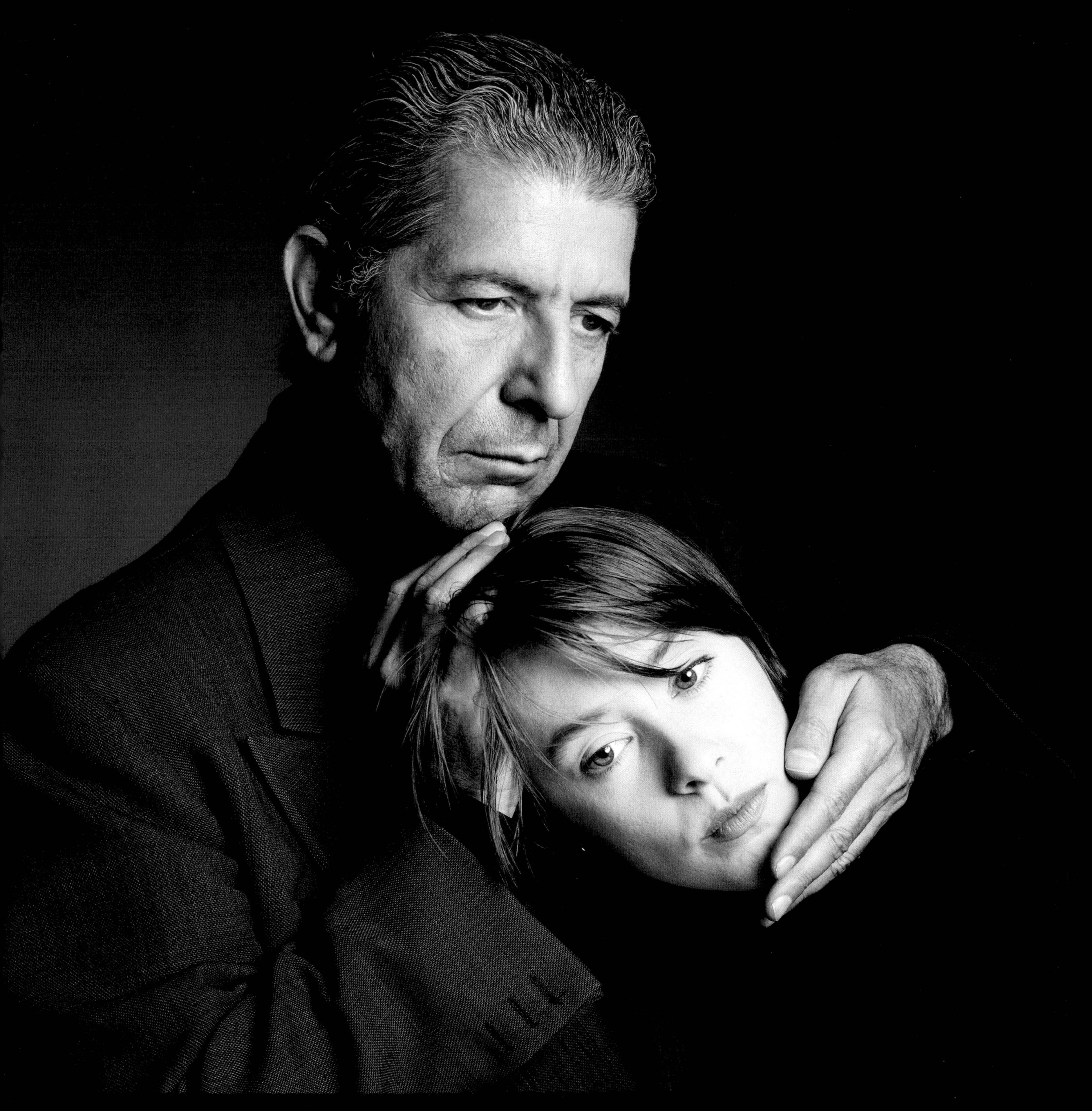

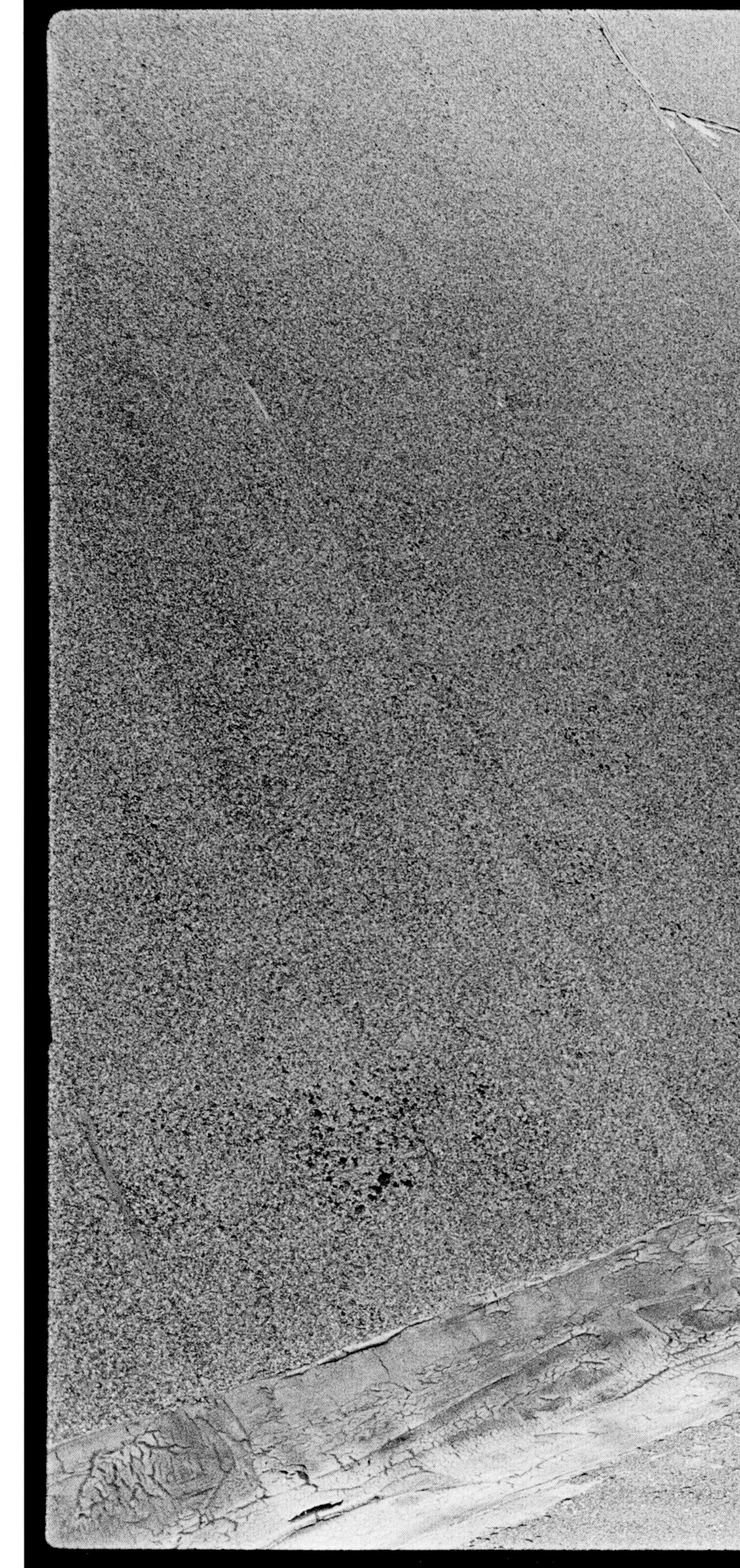

THIS SPREAD: BRIAN ENO, 1981
FOLLOWING SPREAD: AL GREEN, 1982

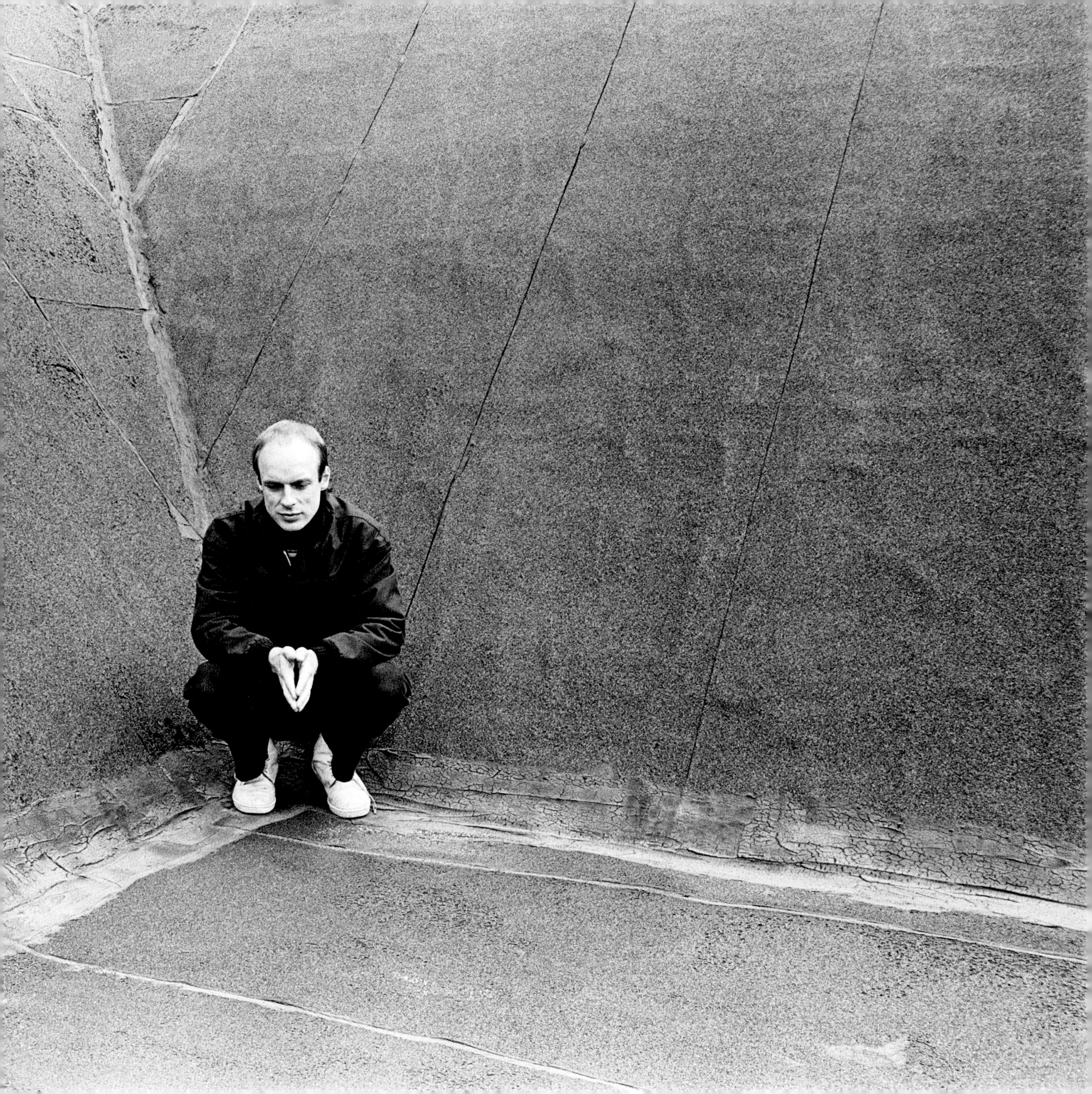

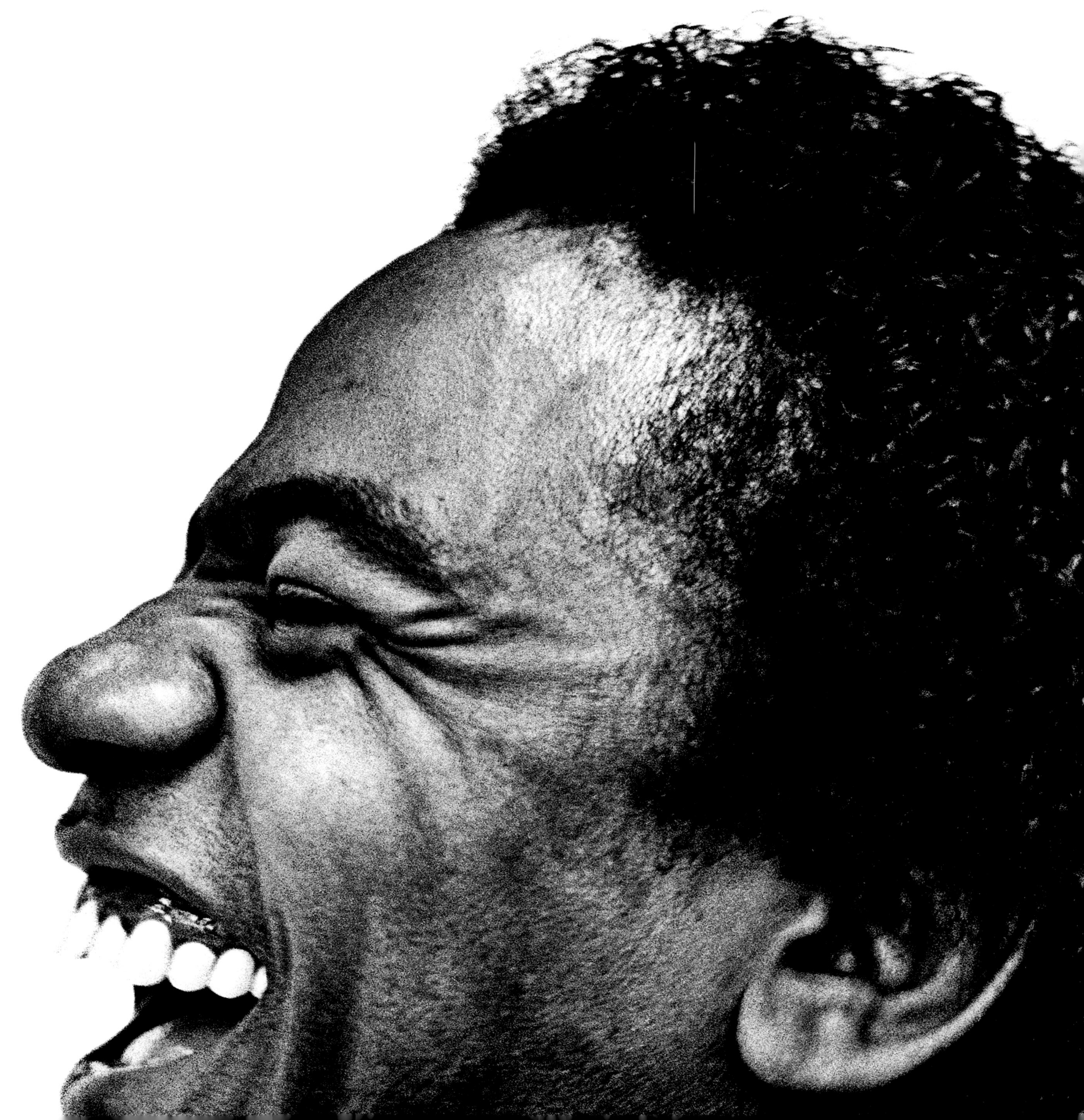

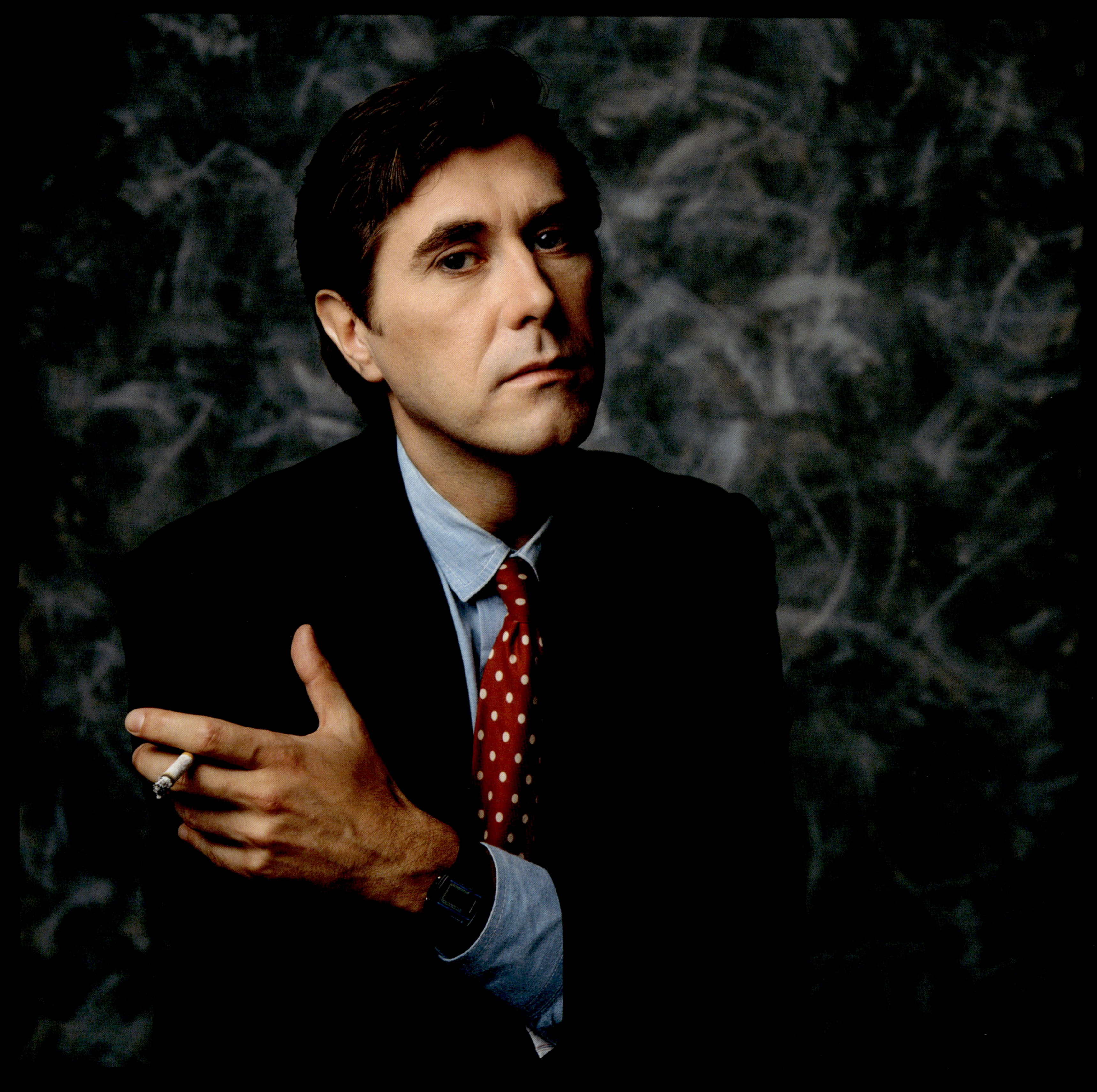

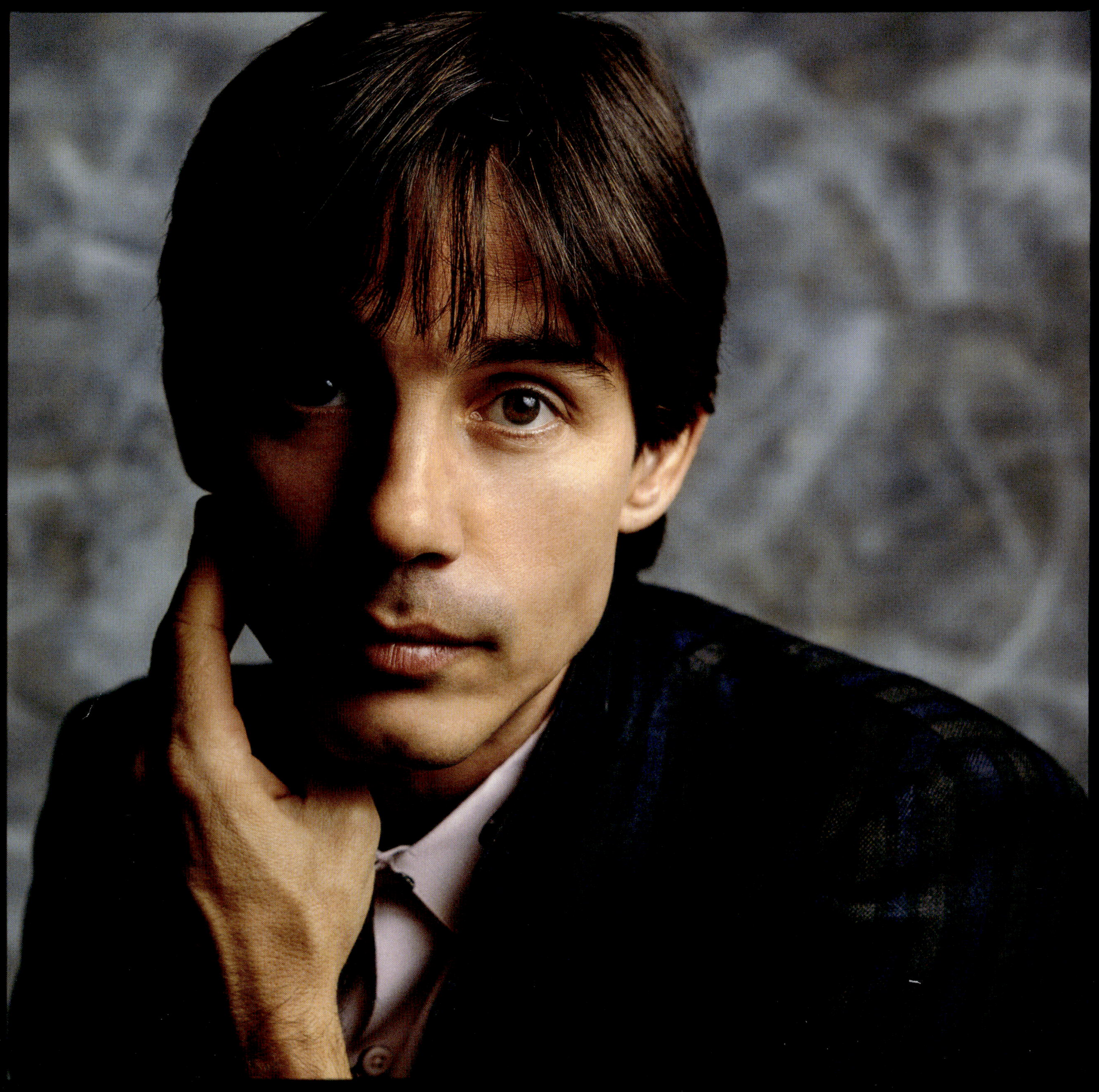

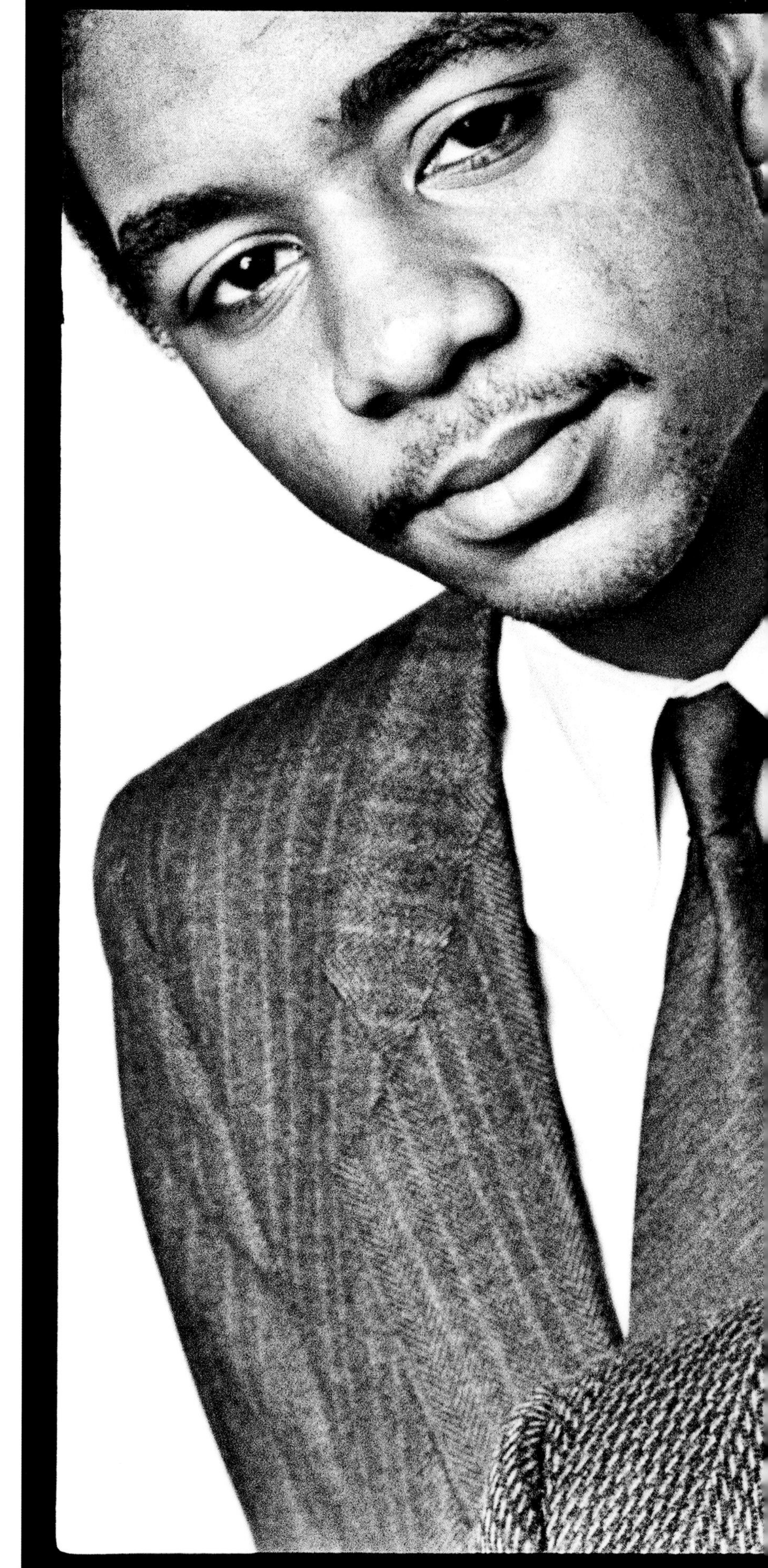

PAGE 66: BRYAN FERRY, 1983; PAGE 67: JACKSON BROWNE, 1983
THIS SPREAD: BRANFORD AND WYNTON MARSALIS, 1982
FOLLOWING SPREAD: MARY J. BLIGE, 1997

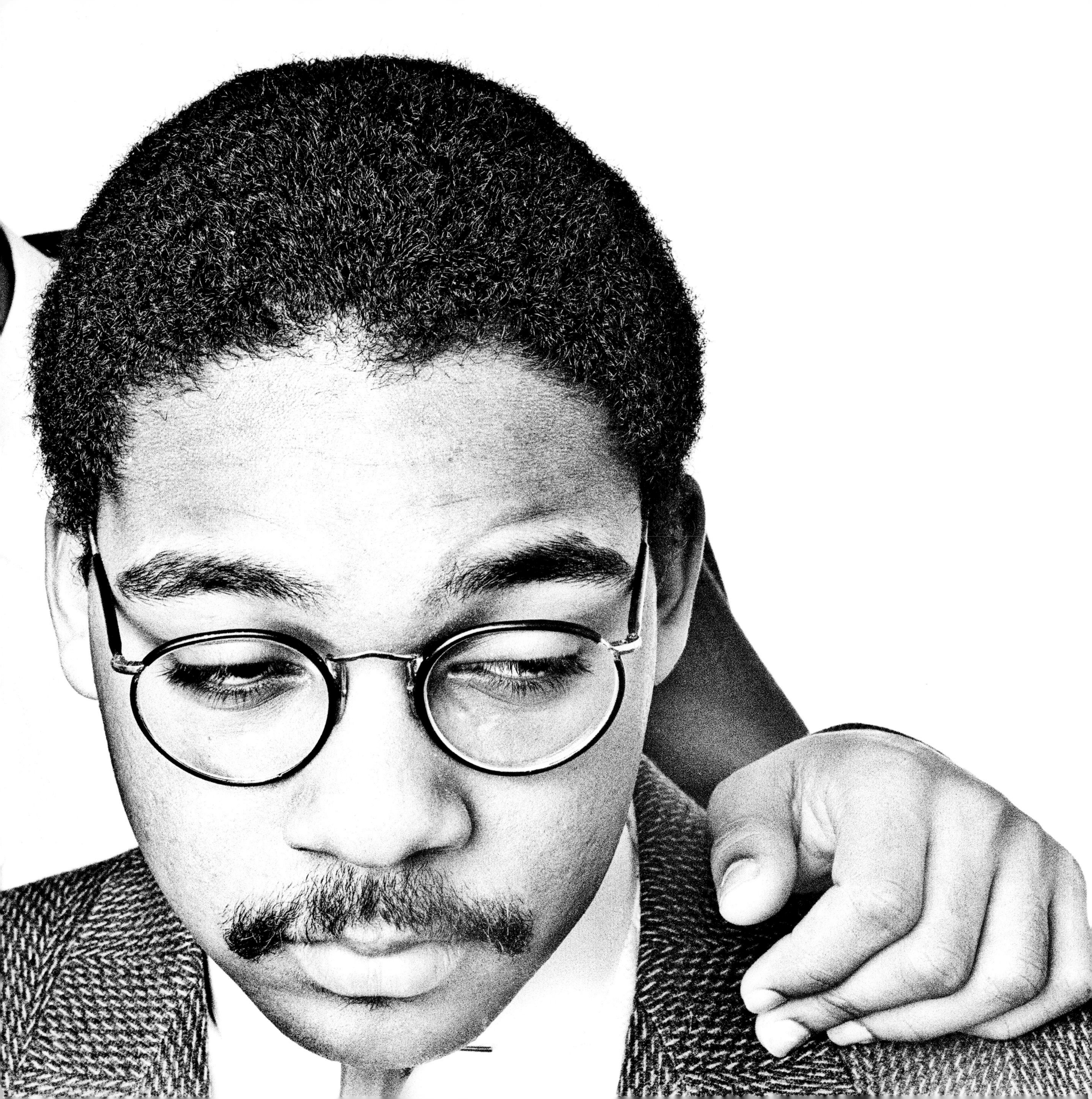

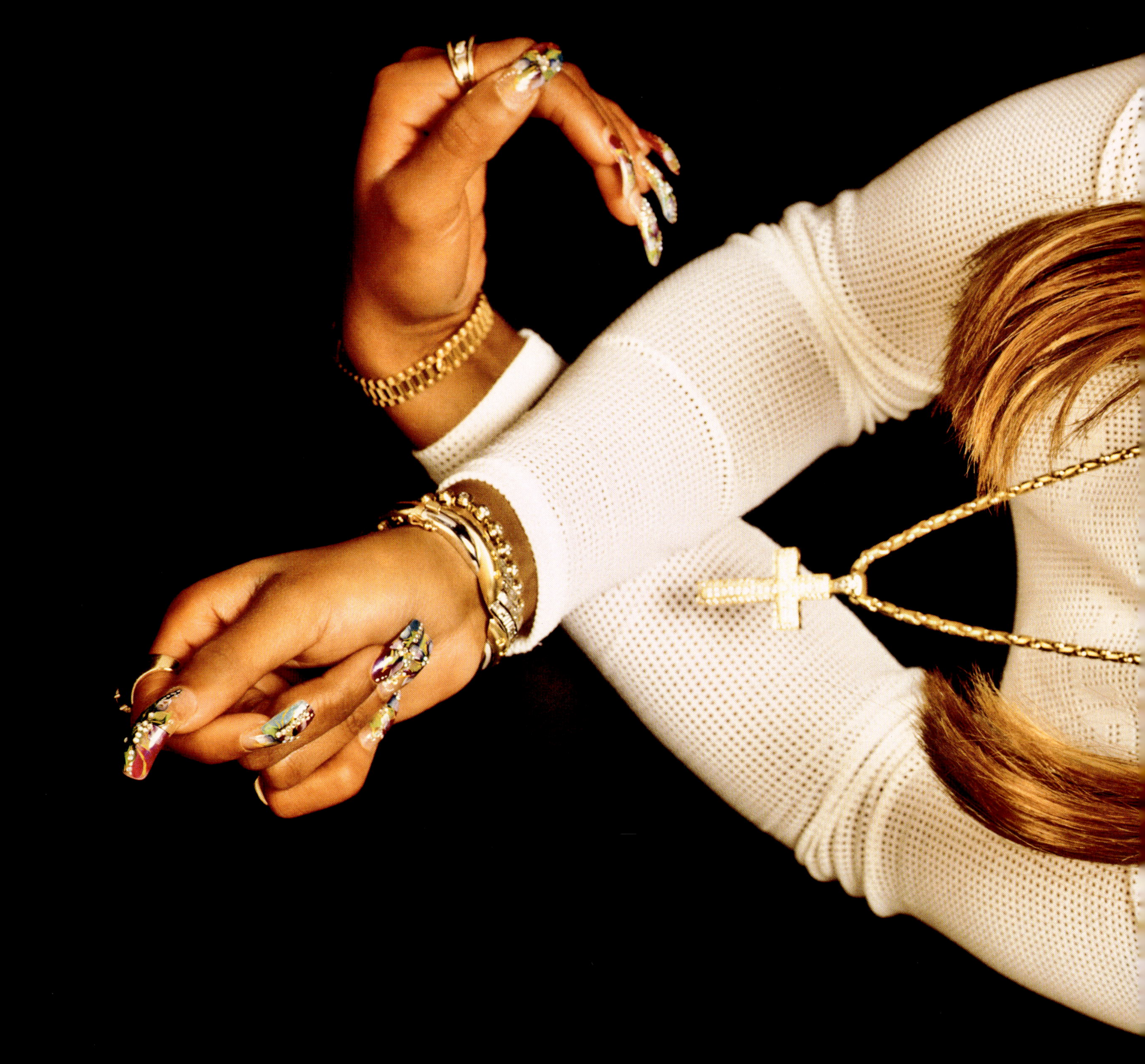

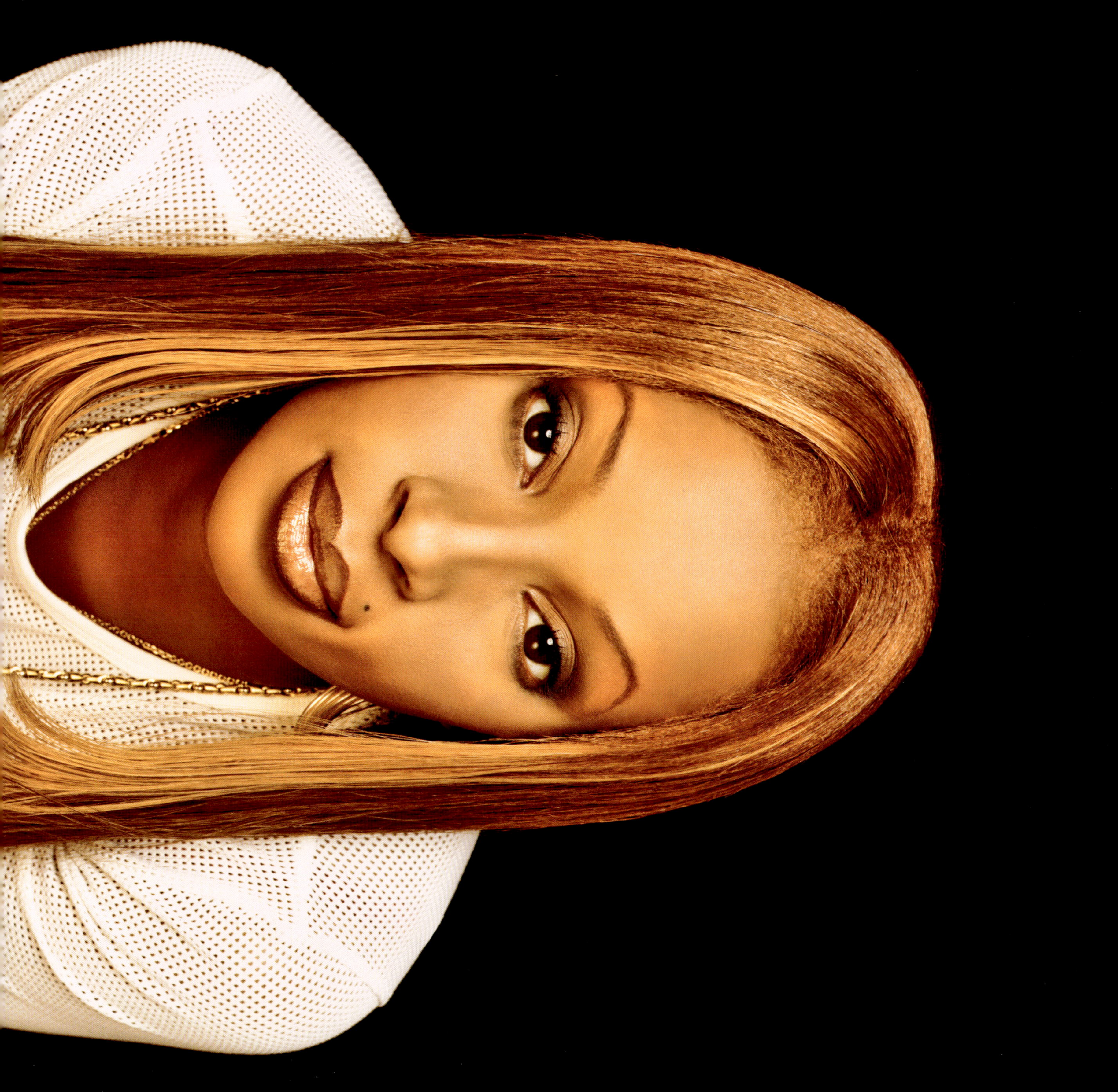

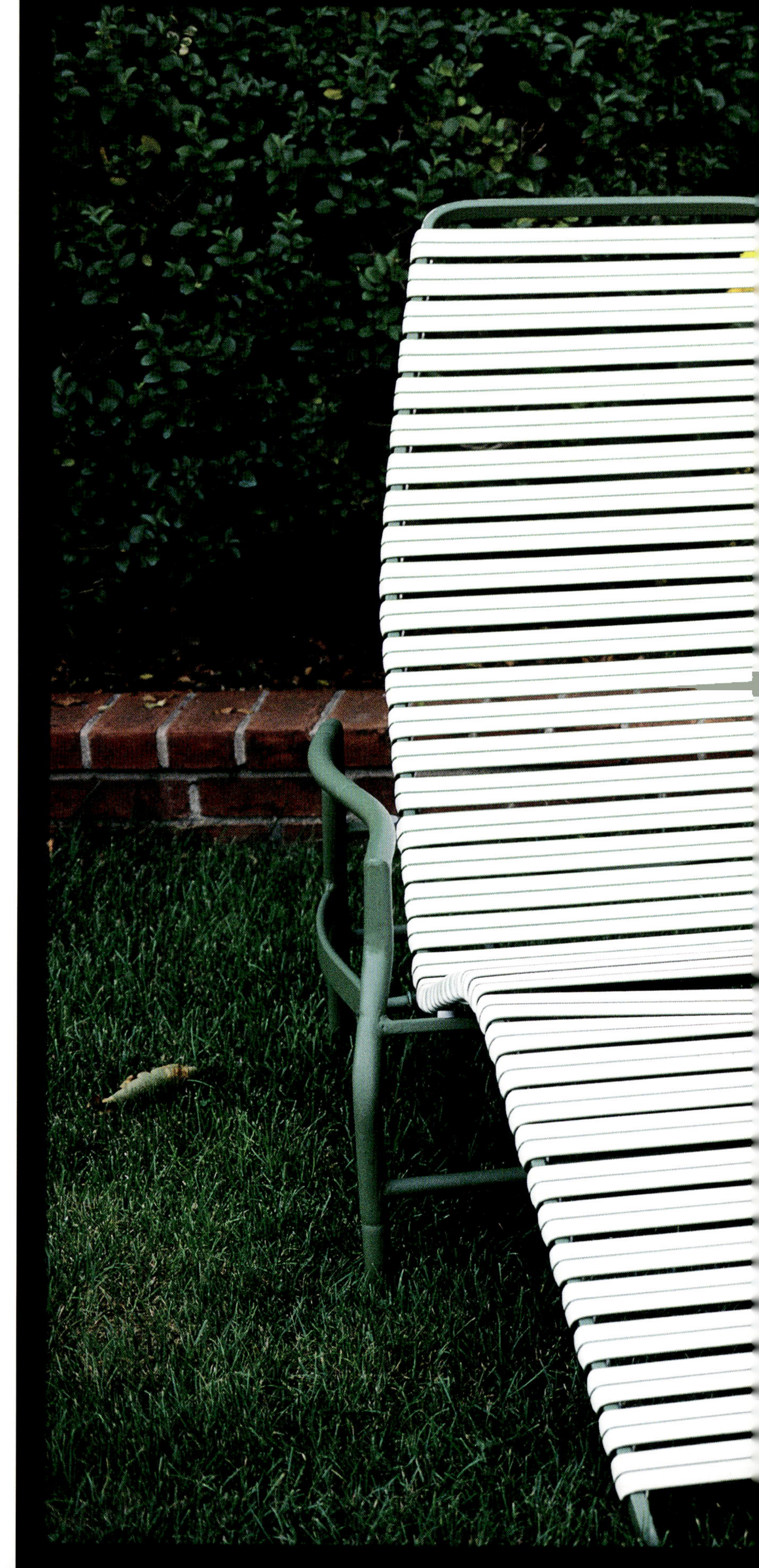

BILLY JOEL, 1982

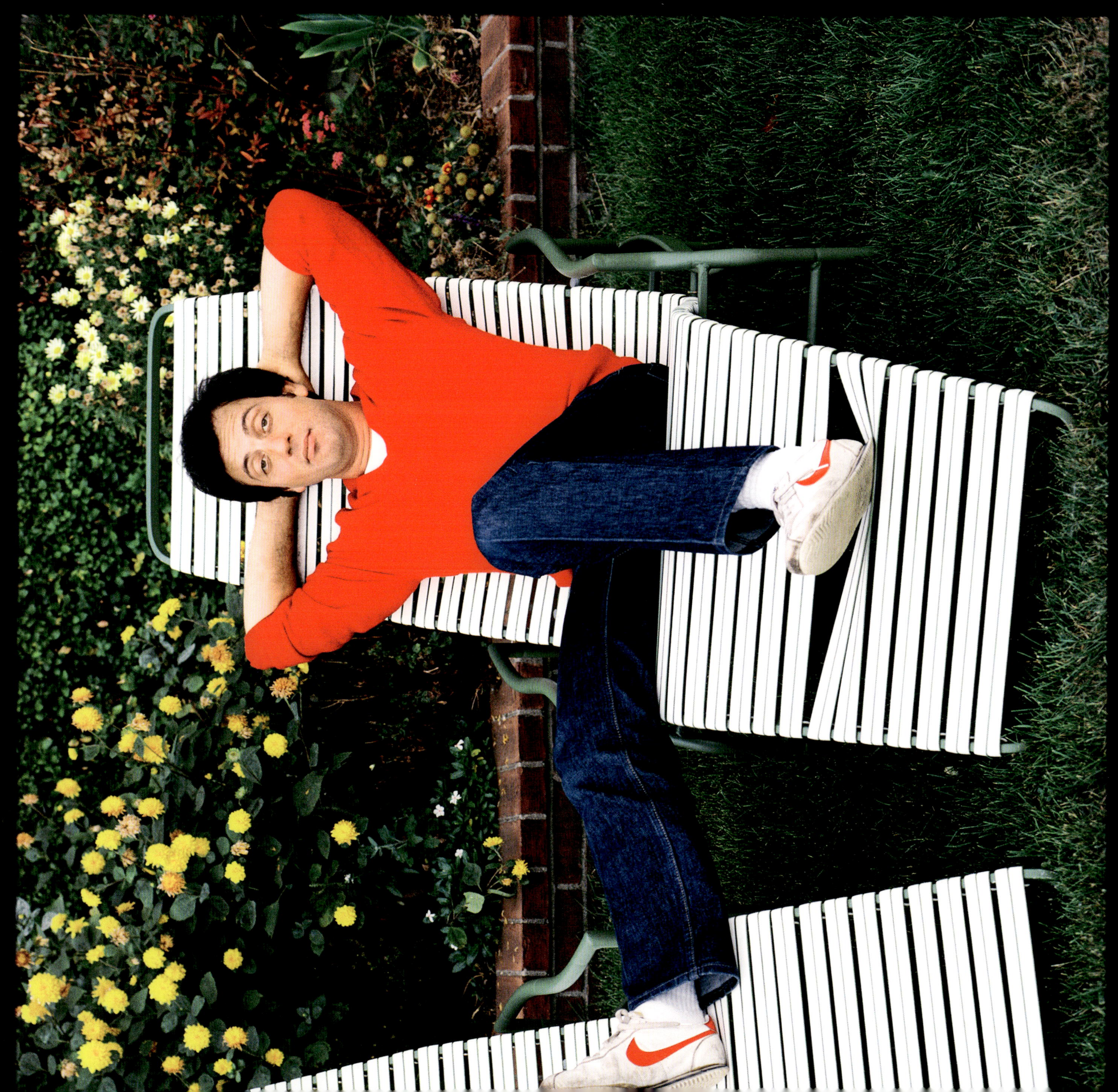

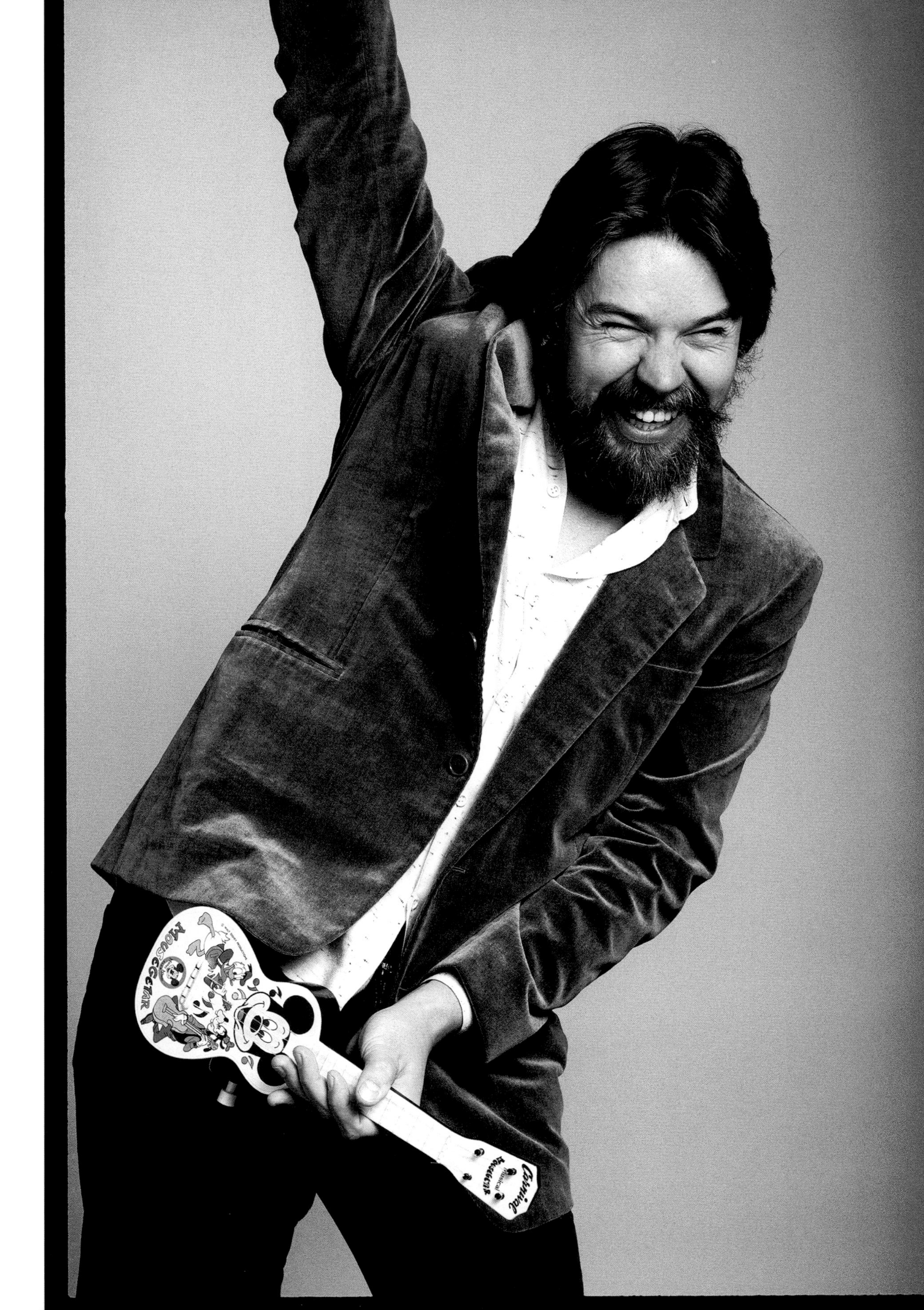

BOB SEGER, 1982;
OPPOSITE:
JUDY COLLINS, 1990

74

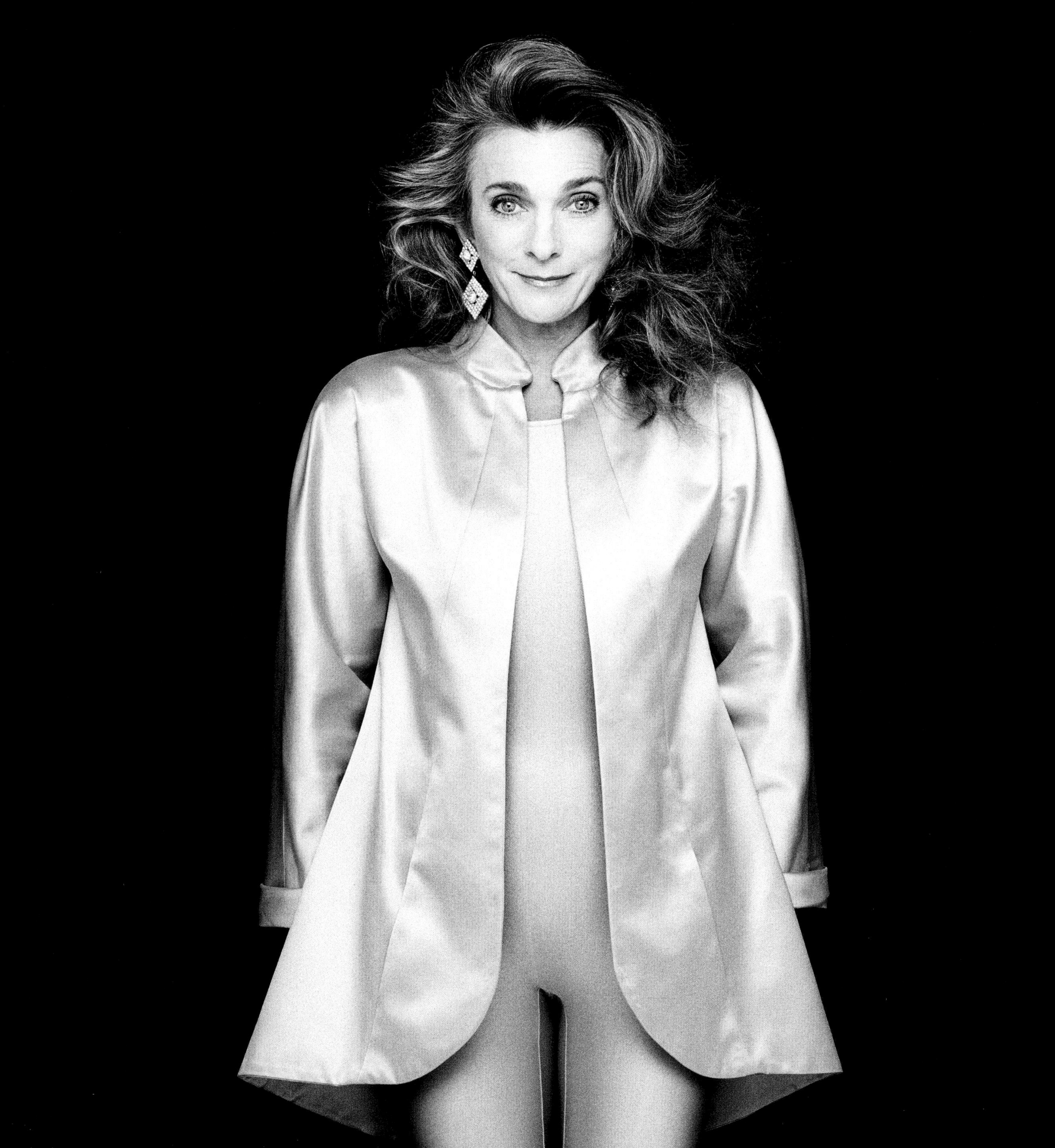

THIS SPREAD: DWIGHT TWILLEY, 1982
PAGE 78: SINÉAD O'CONNOR, 1990; PAGE 79: ROBERT FRIPP, 1985

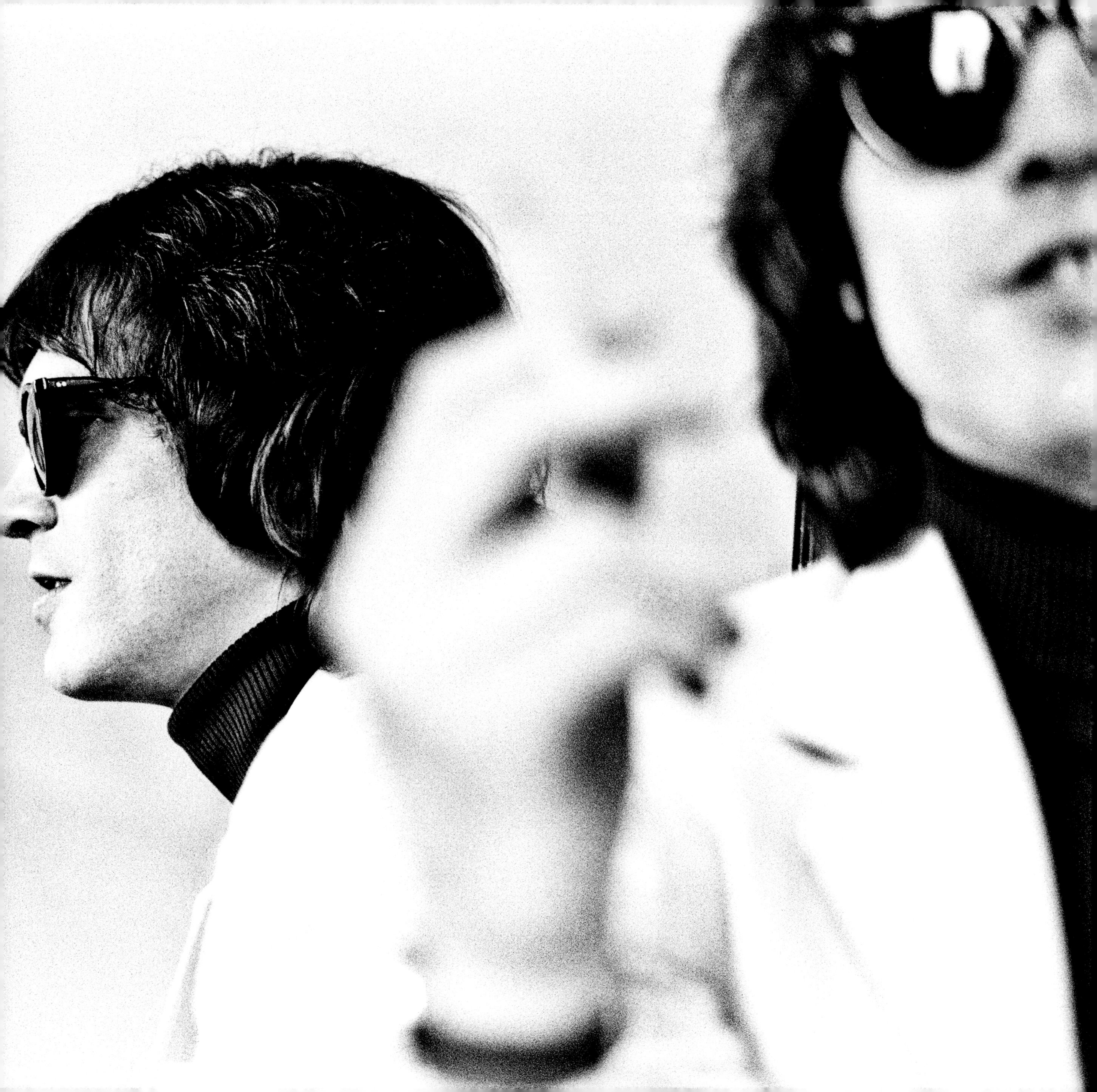

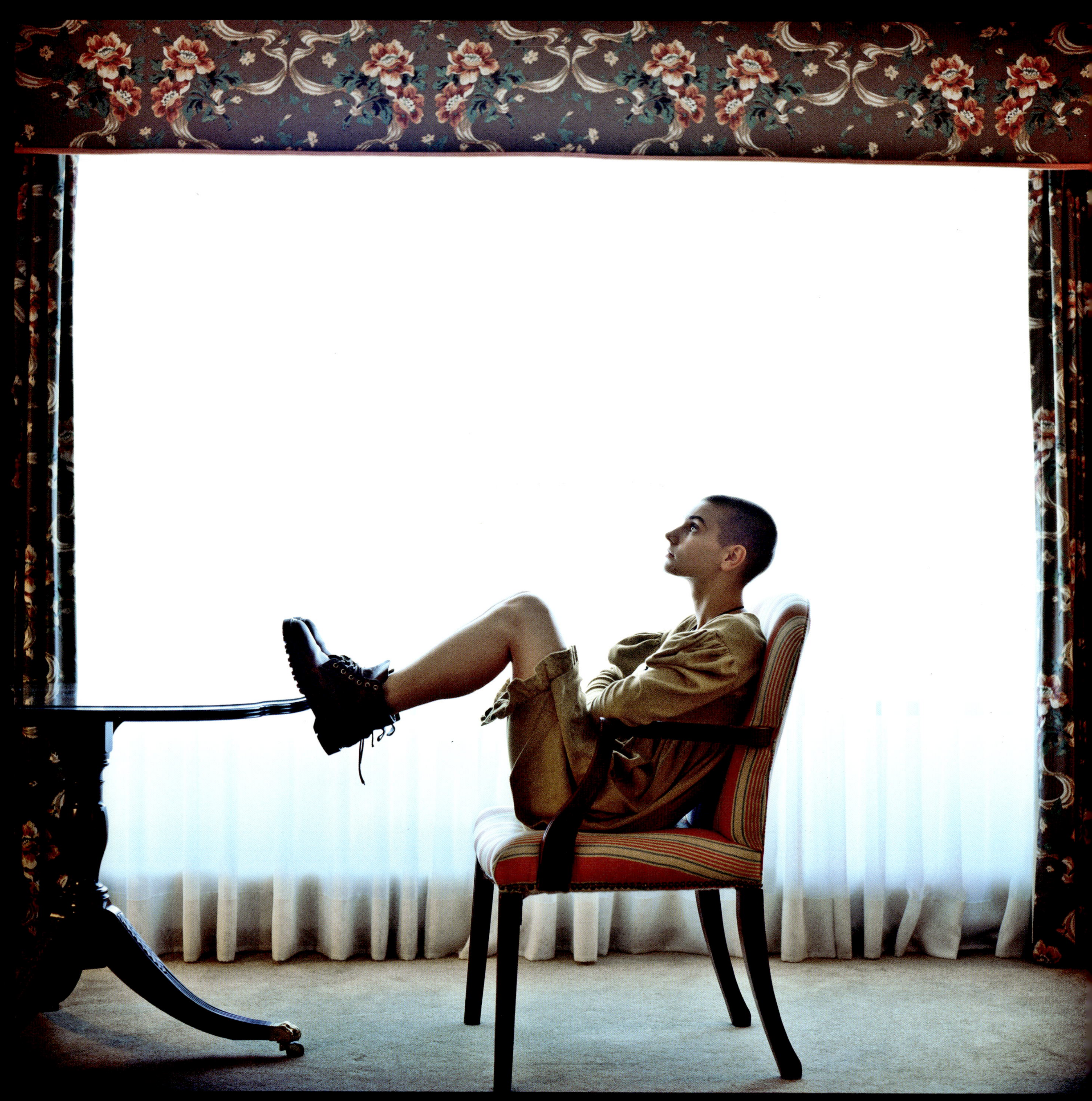

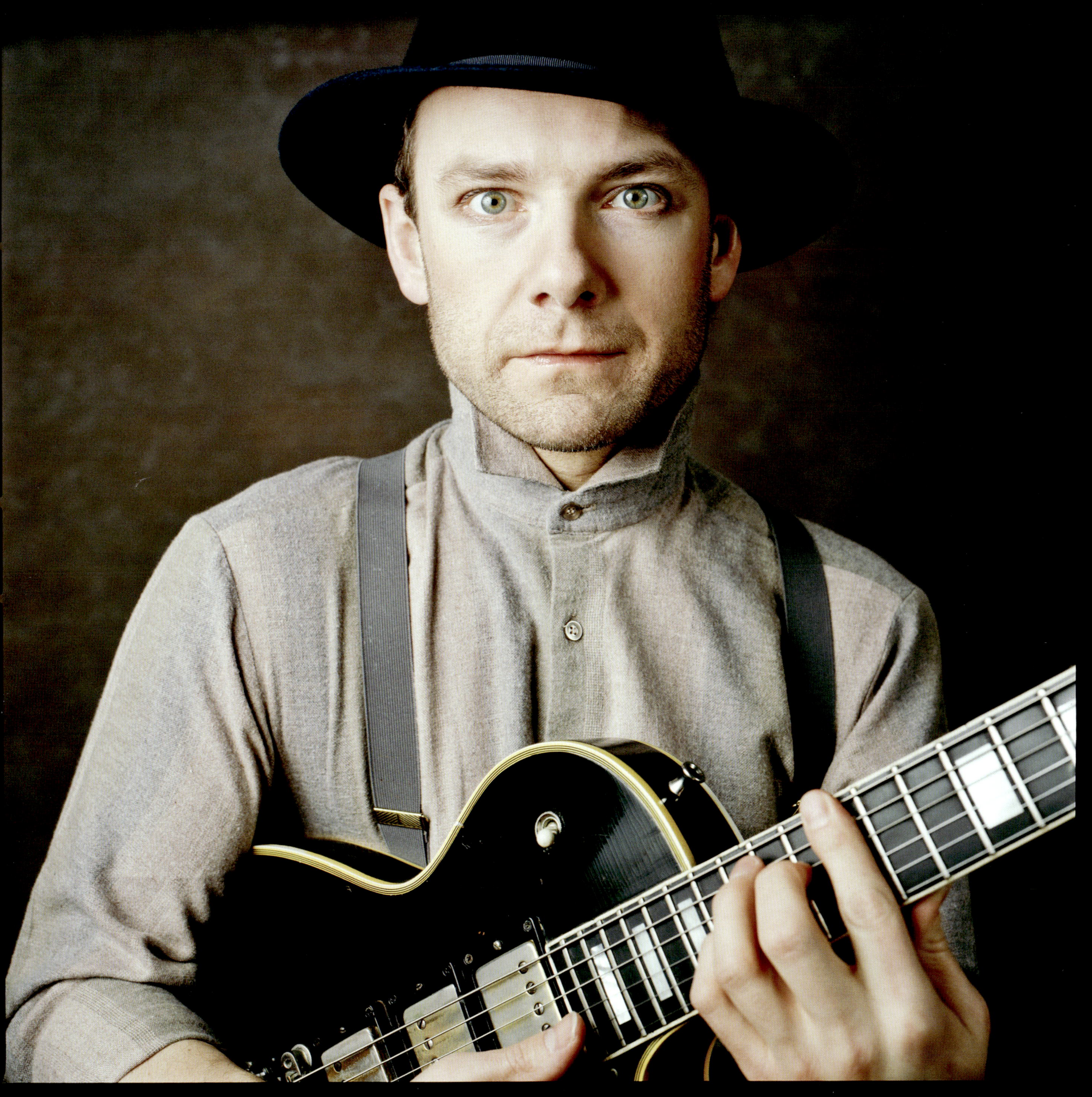

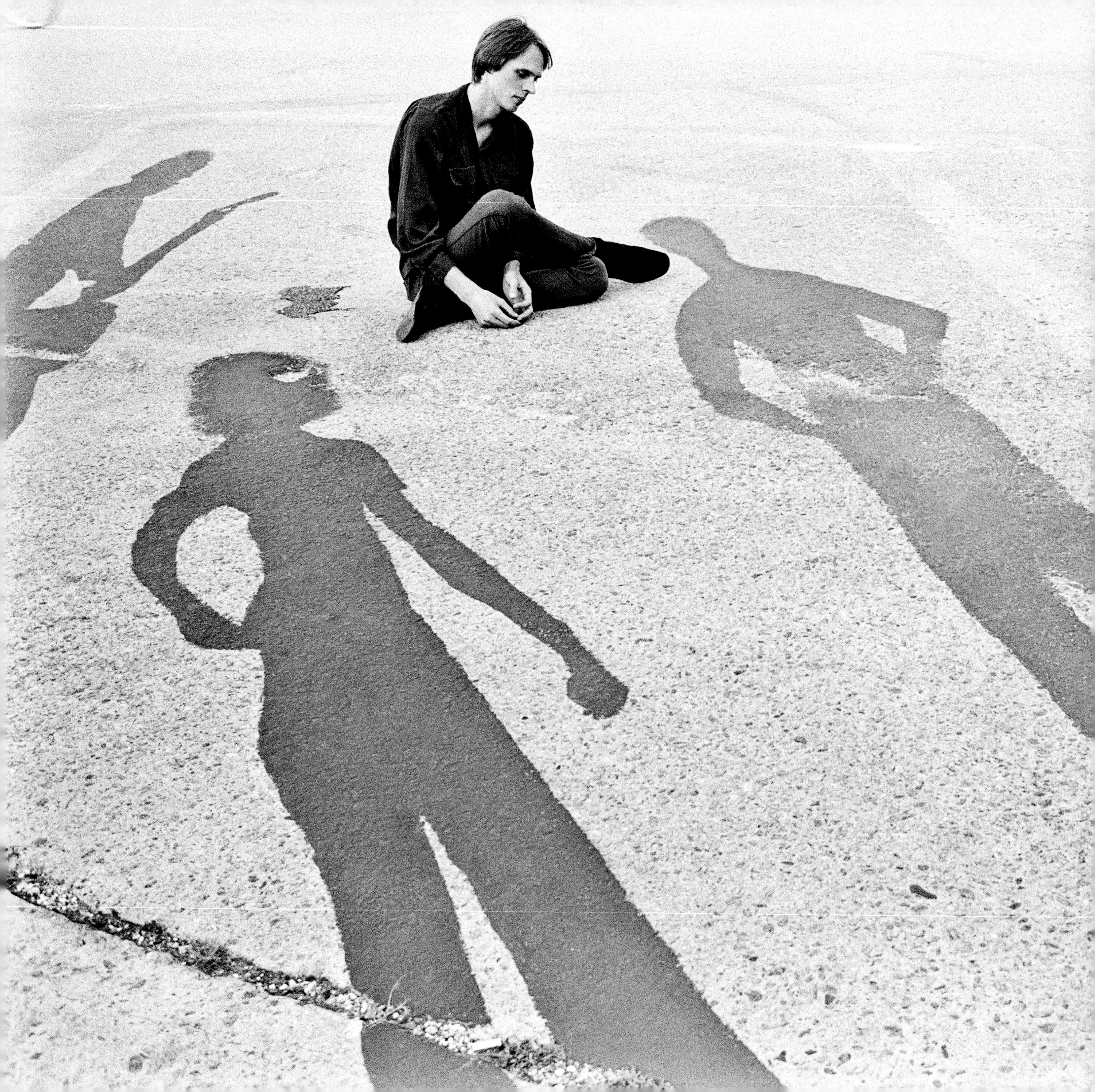

TOM VERLAINE, 1983

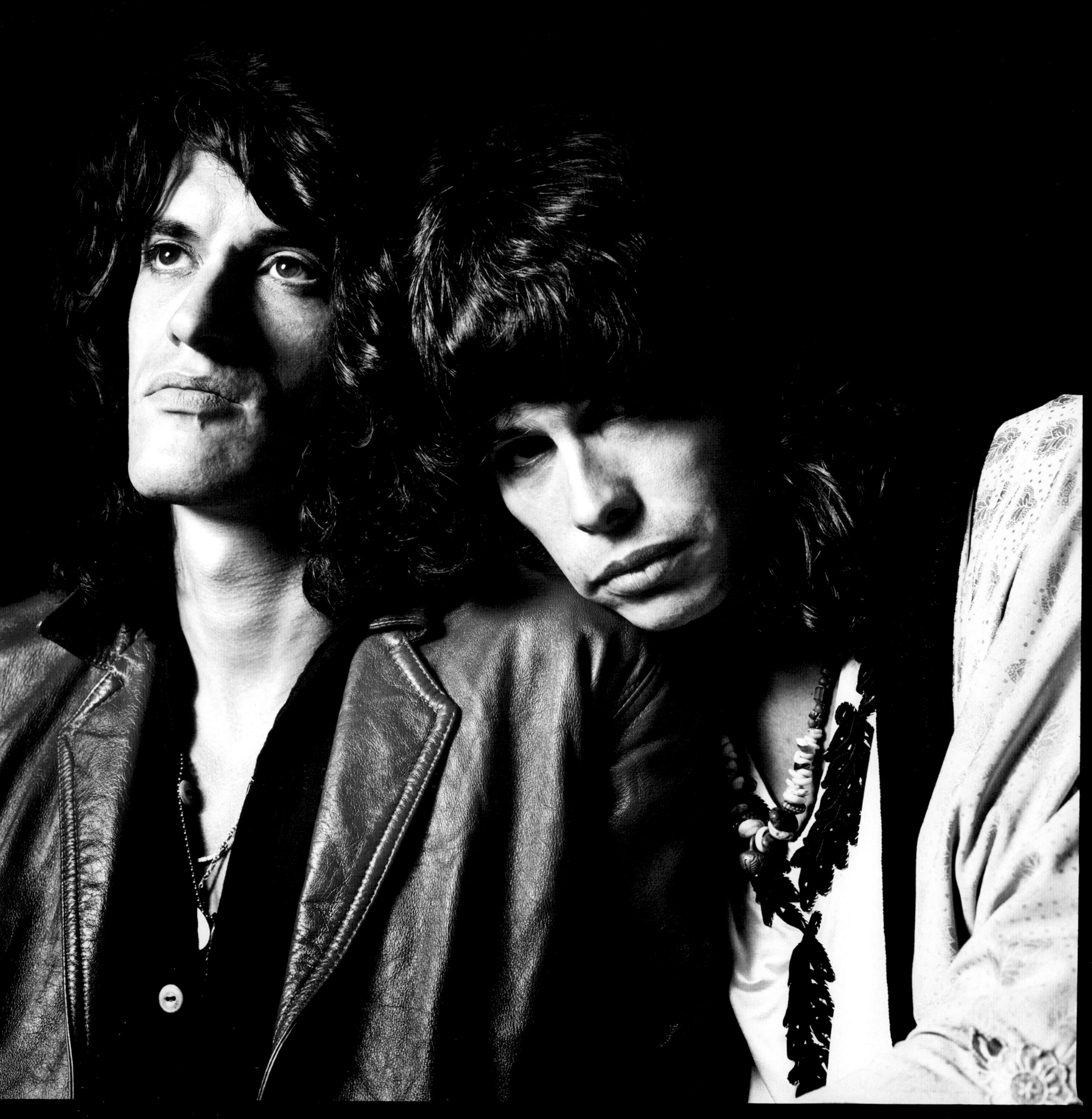

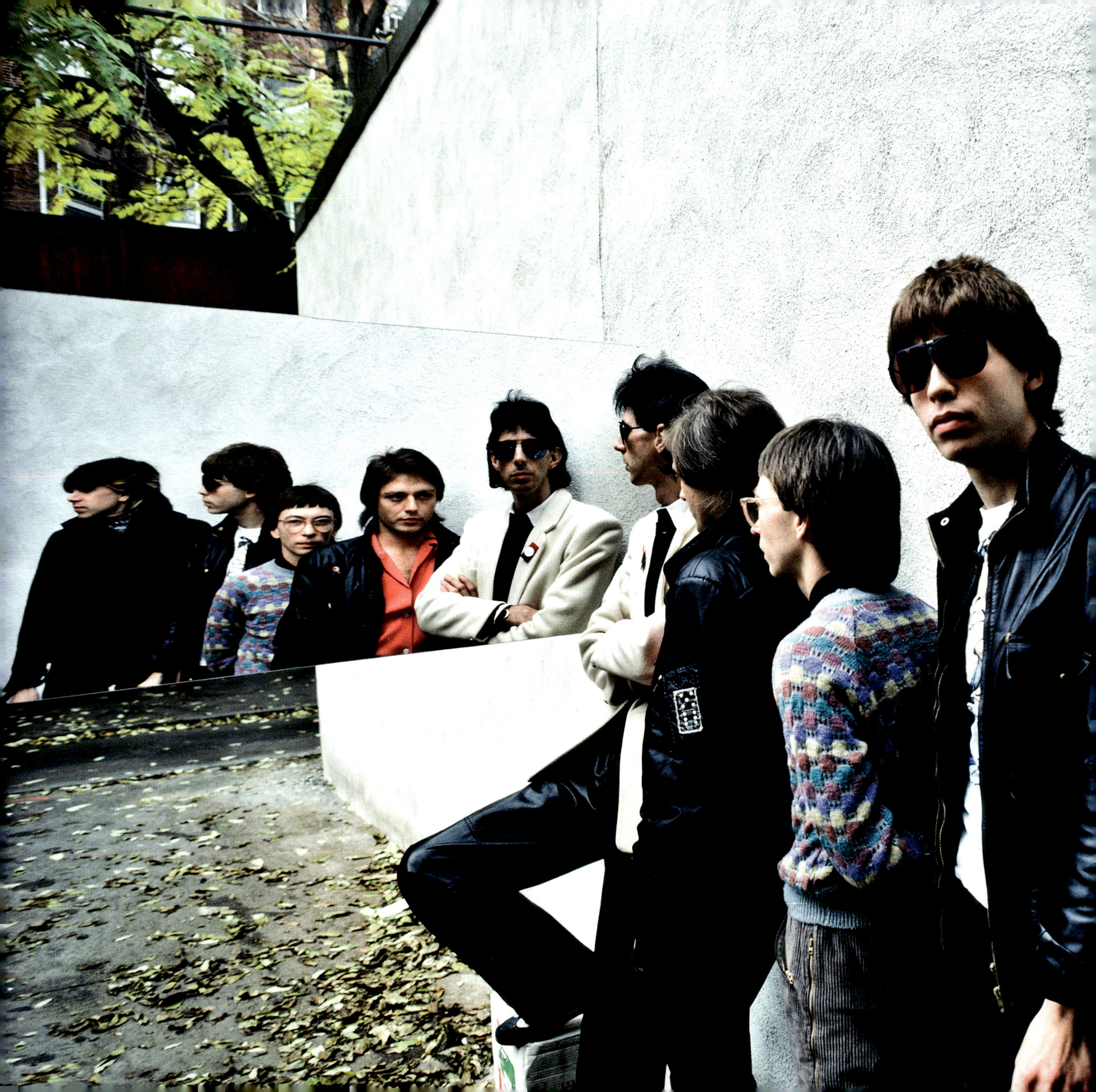

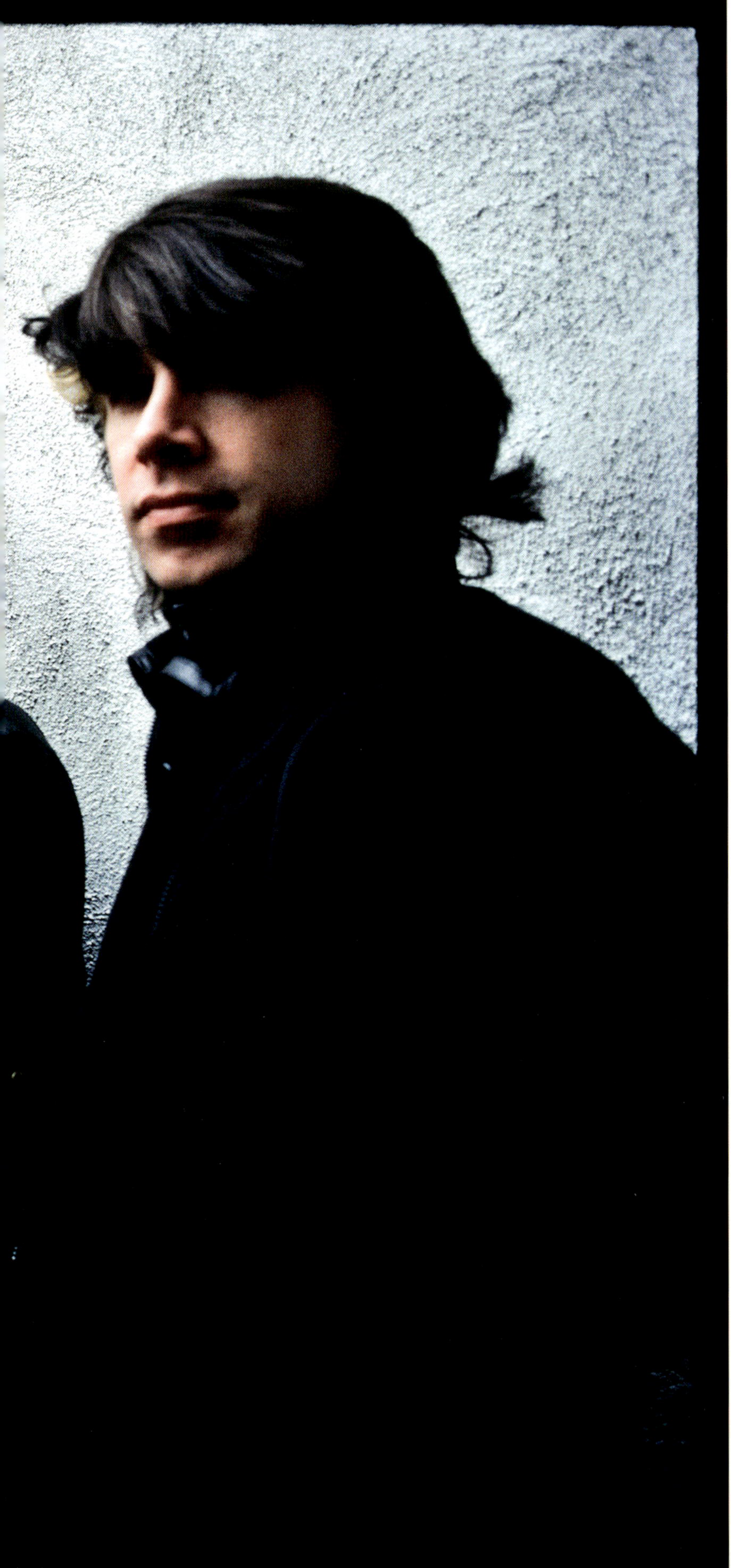

THE CARS, 1981

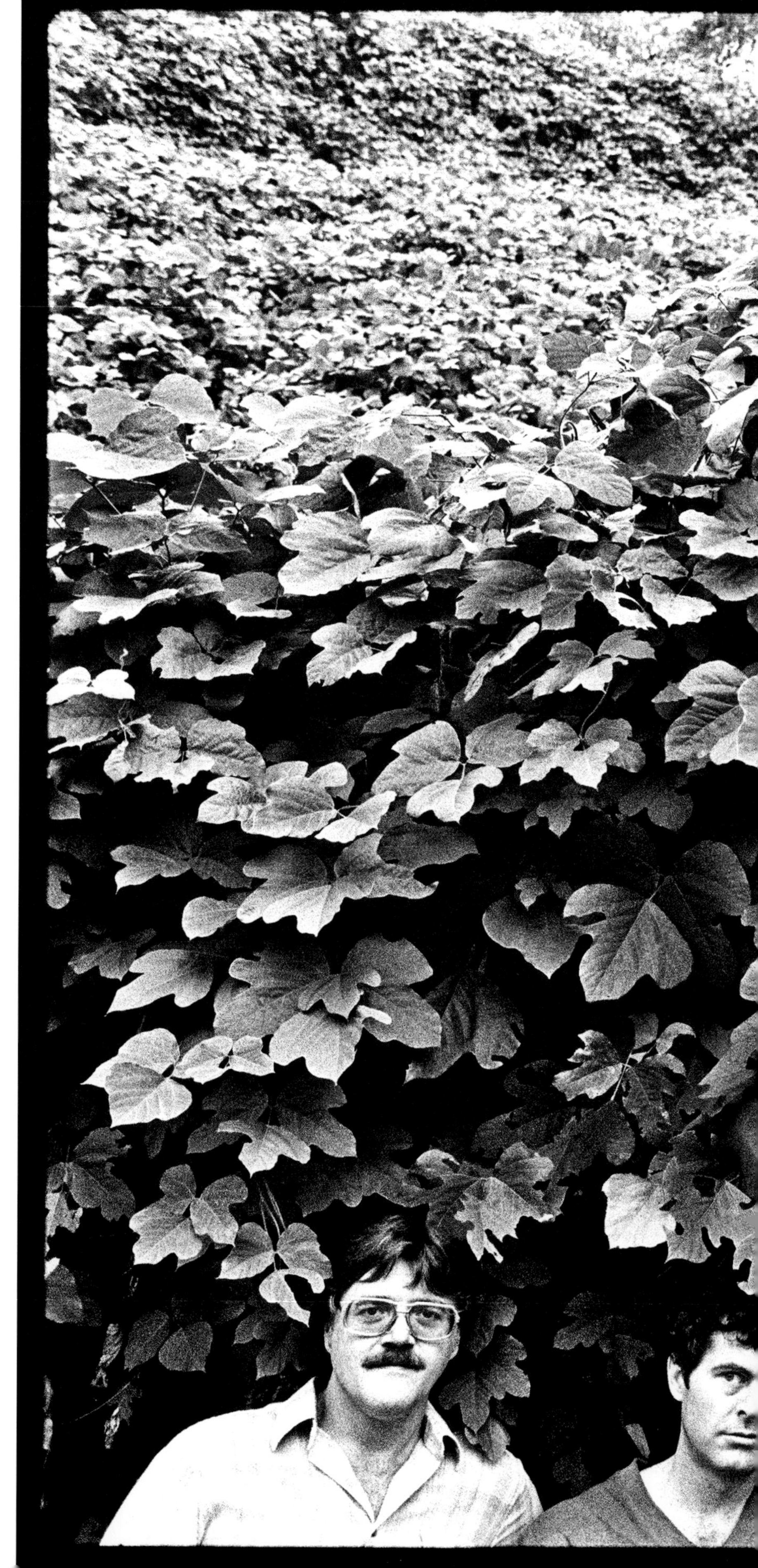

THIS SPREAD: MUSCLE SHOALS RHYTHM SECTION, 1980
PAGE 88: ECHO & THE BUNNYMEN, 1985; PAGE 89: JOHN LYDON, 1985

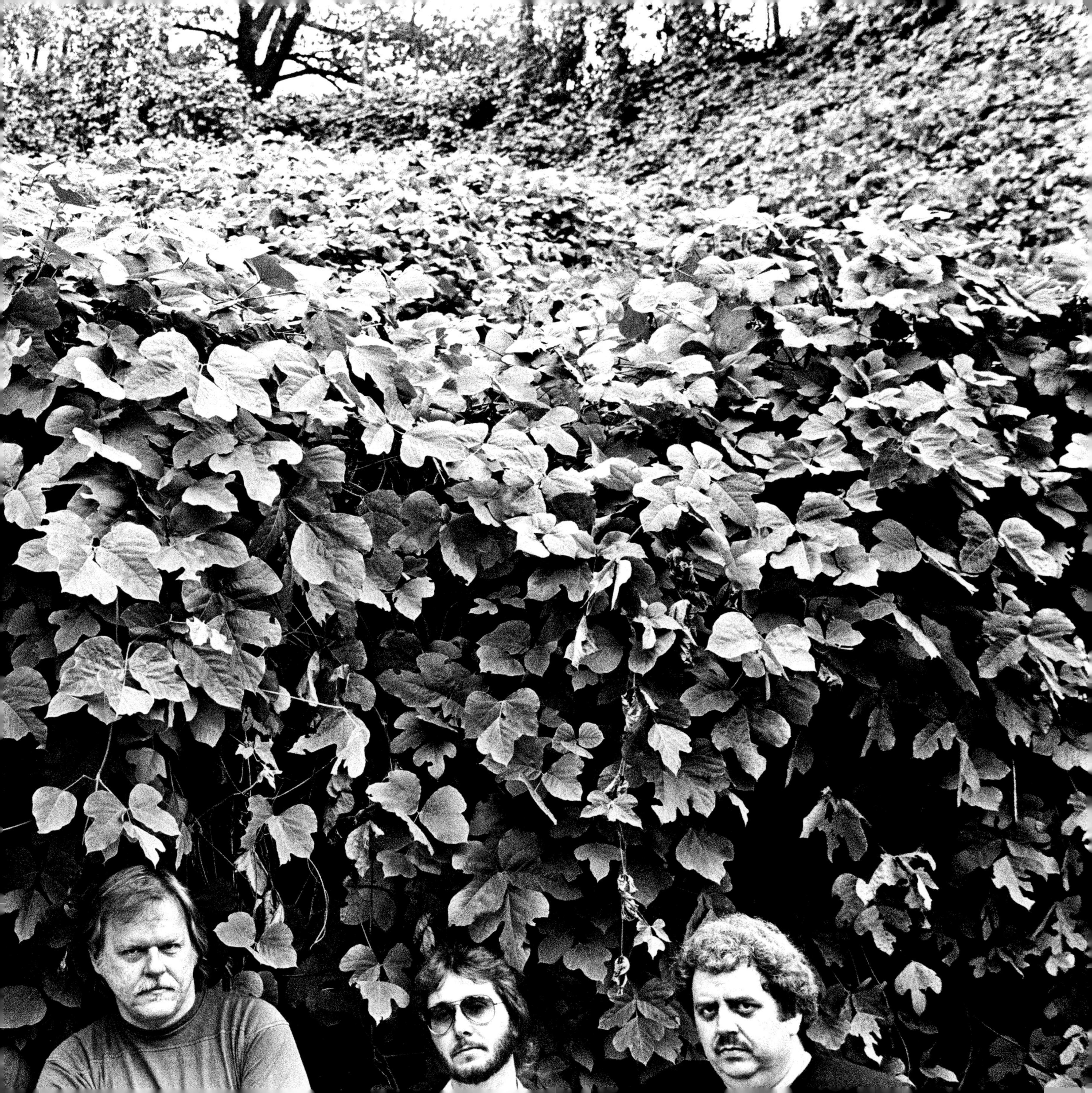

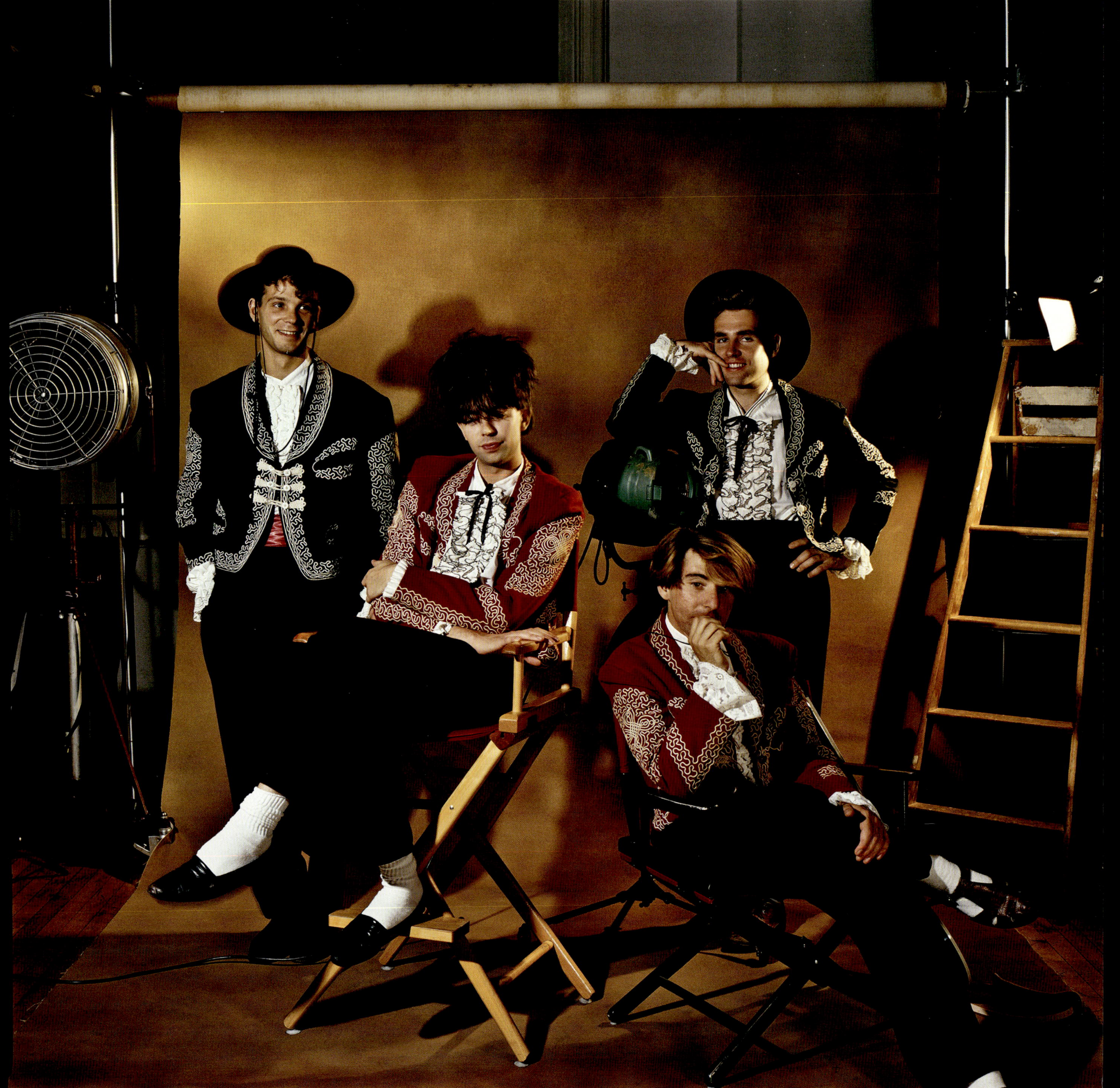

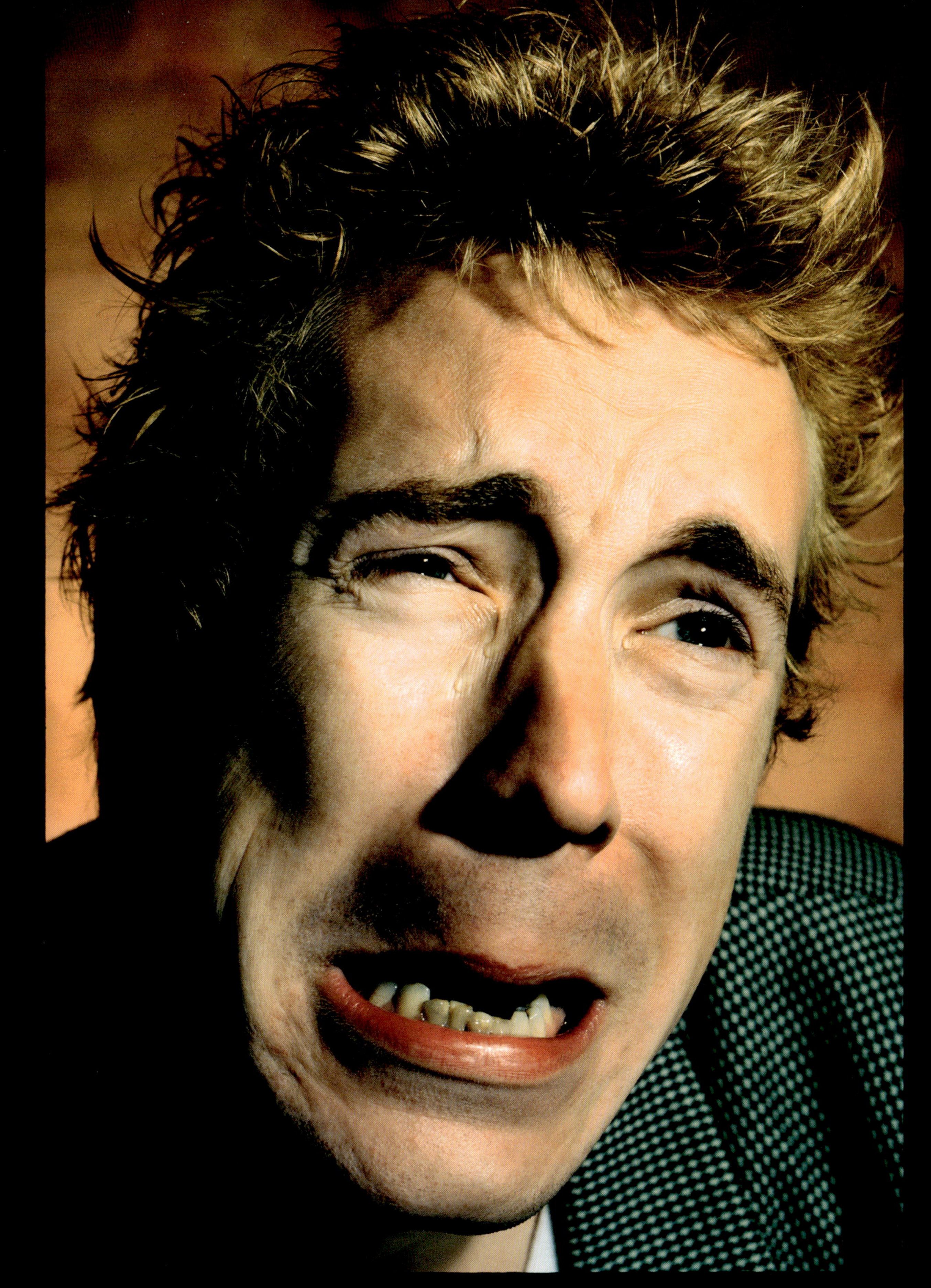

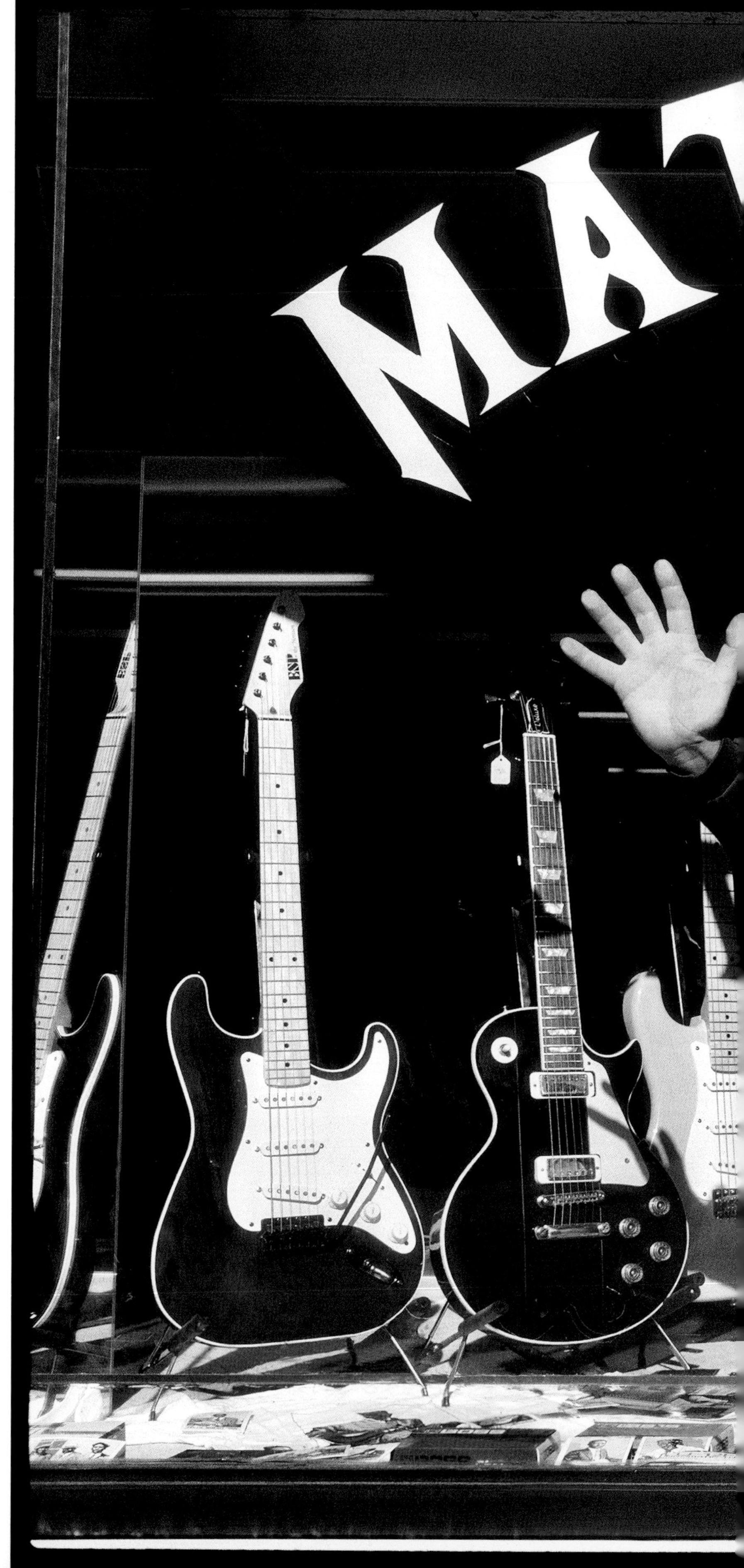

JOHN SEBASTIAN, 1985

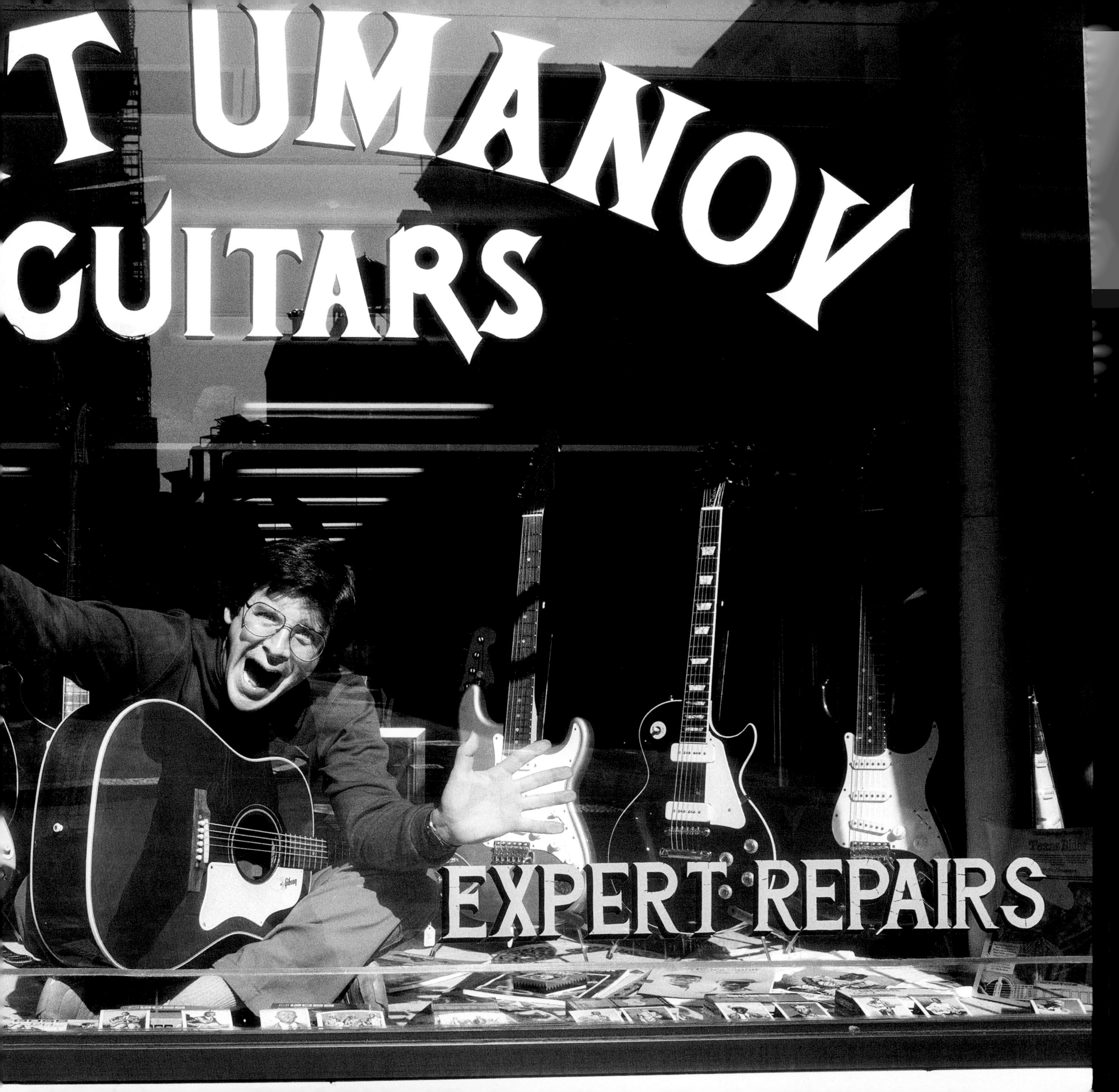

TUMANOV
GUITARS
EXPERT REPAIRS
Gibson

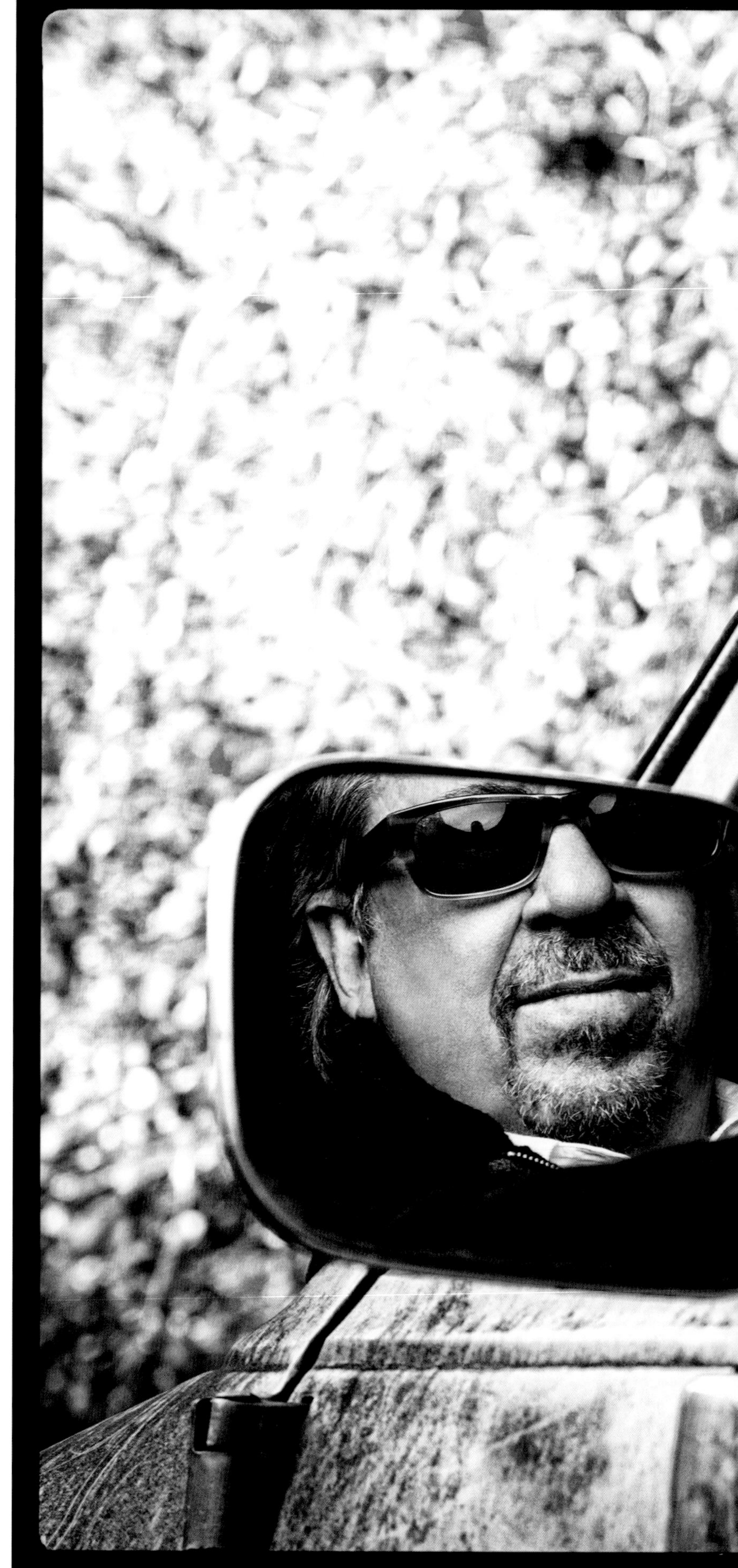

BOZ SCAGGS, 2012

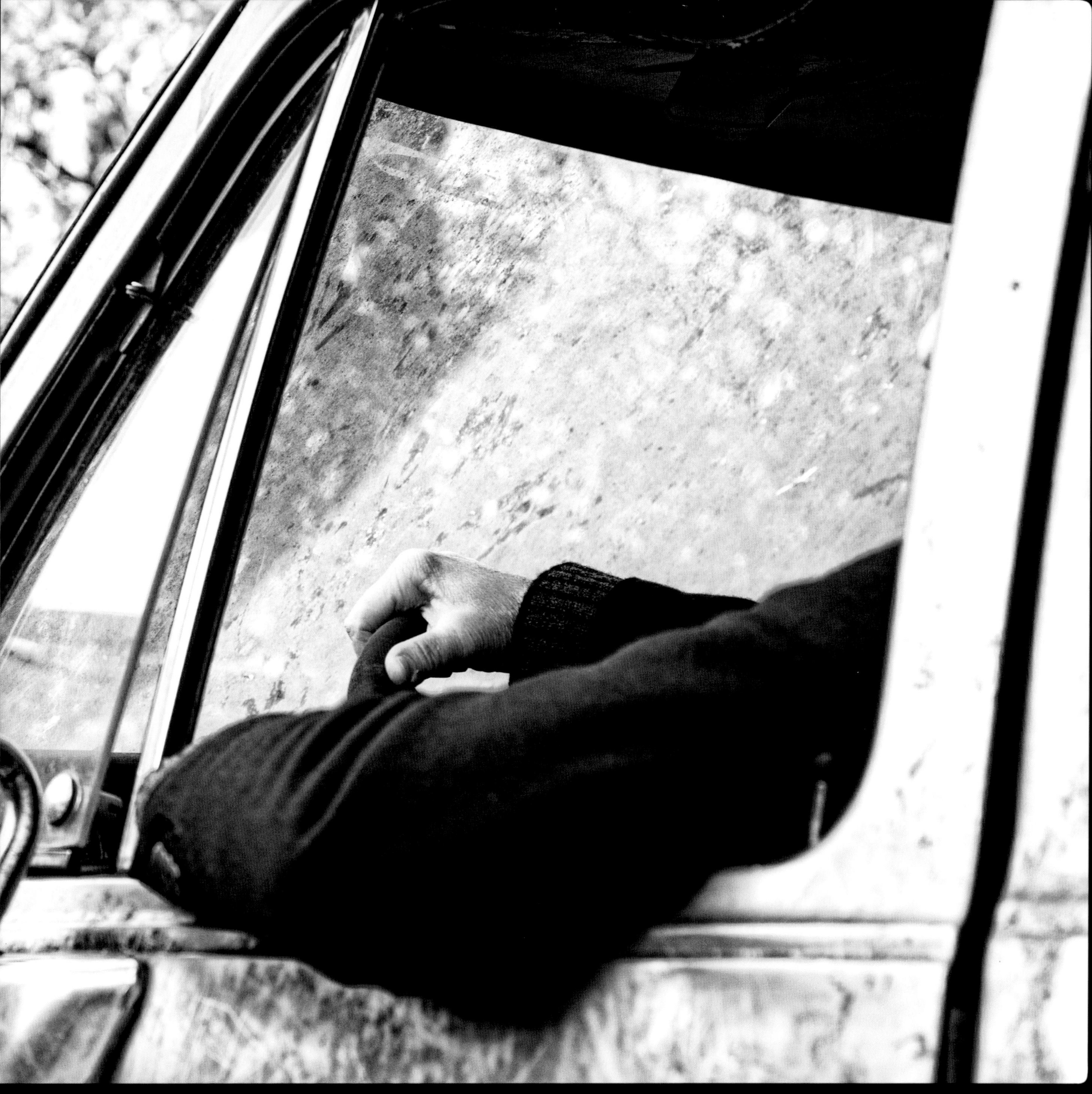

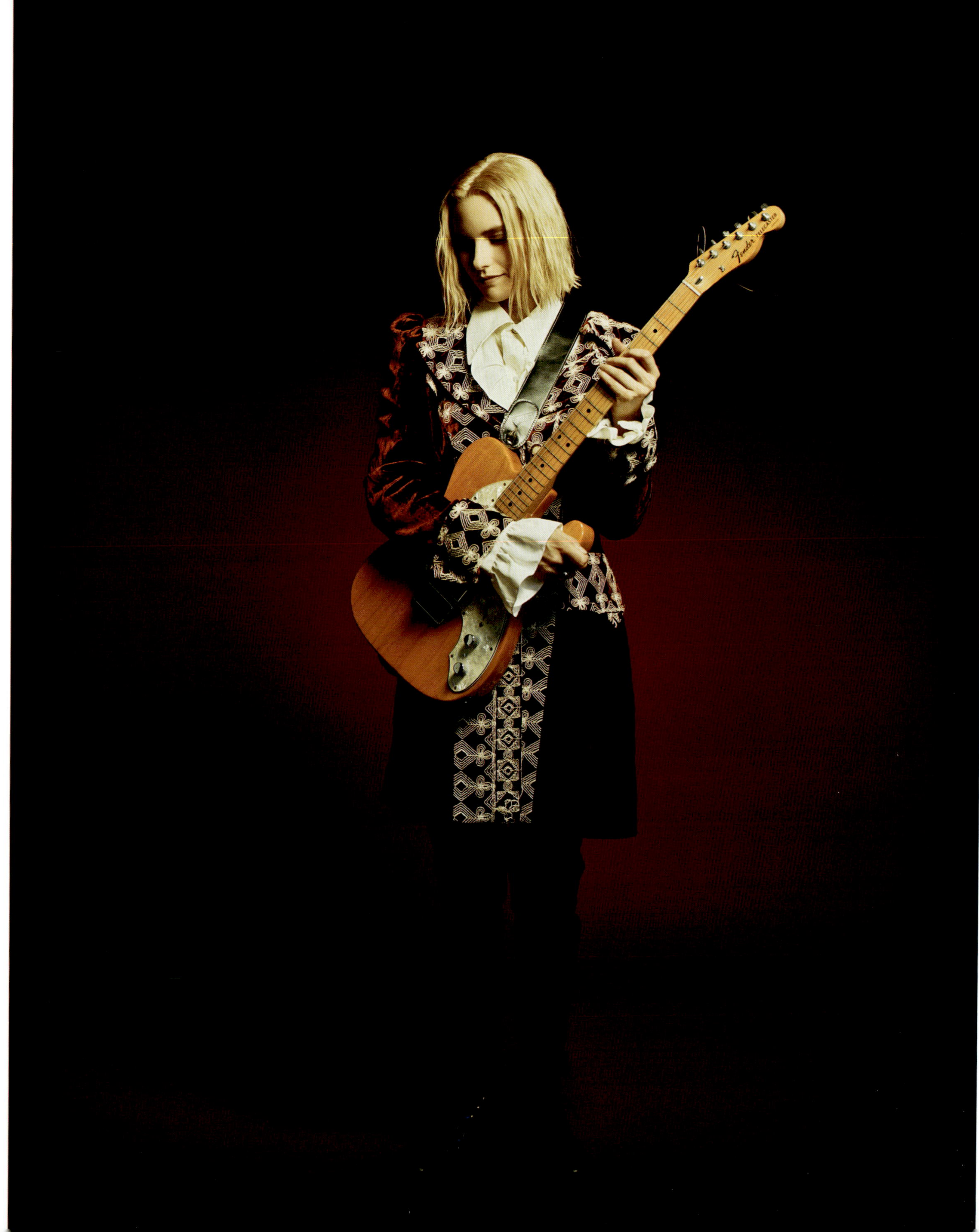

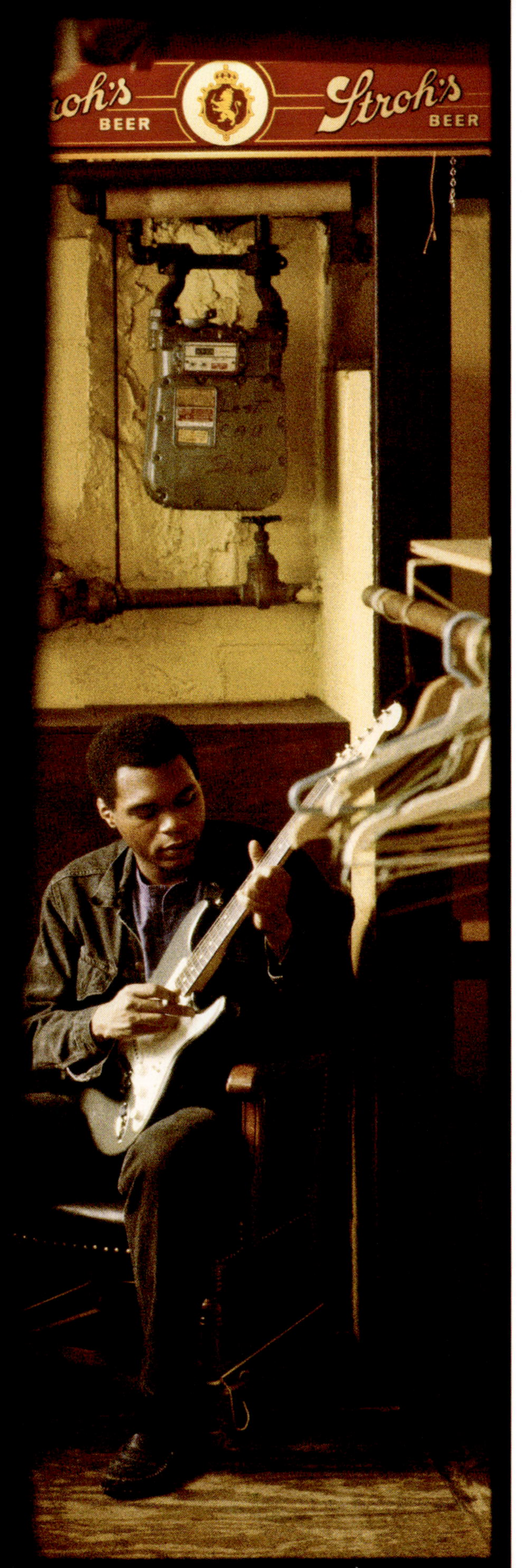

OPPOSITE:
AIMEE MANN, 1993;
THIS PAGE:
ROBERT CRAY, 1987

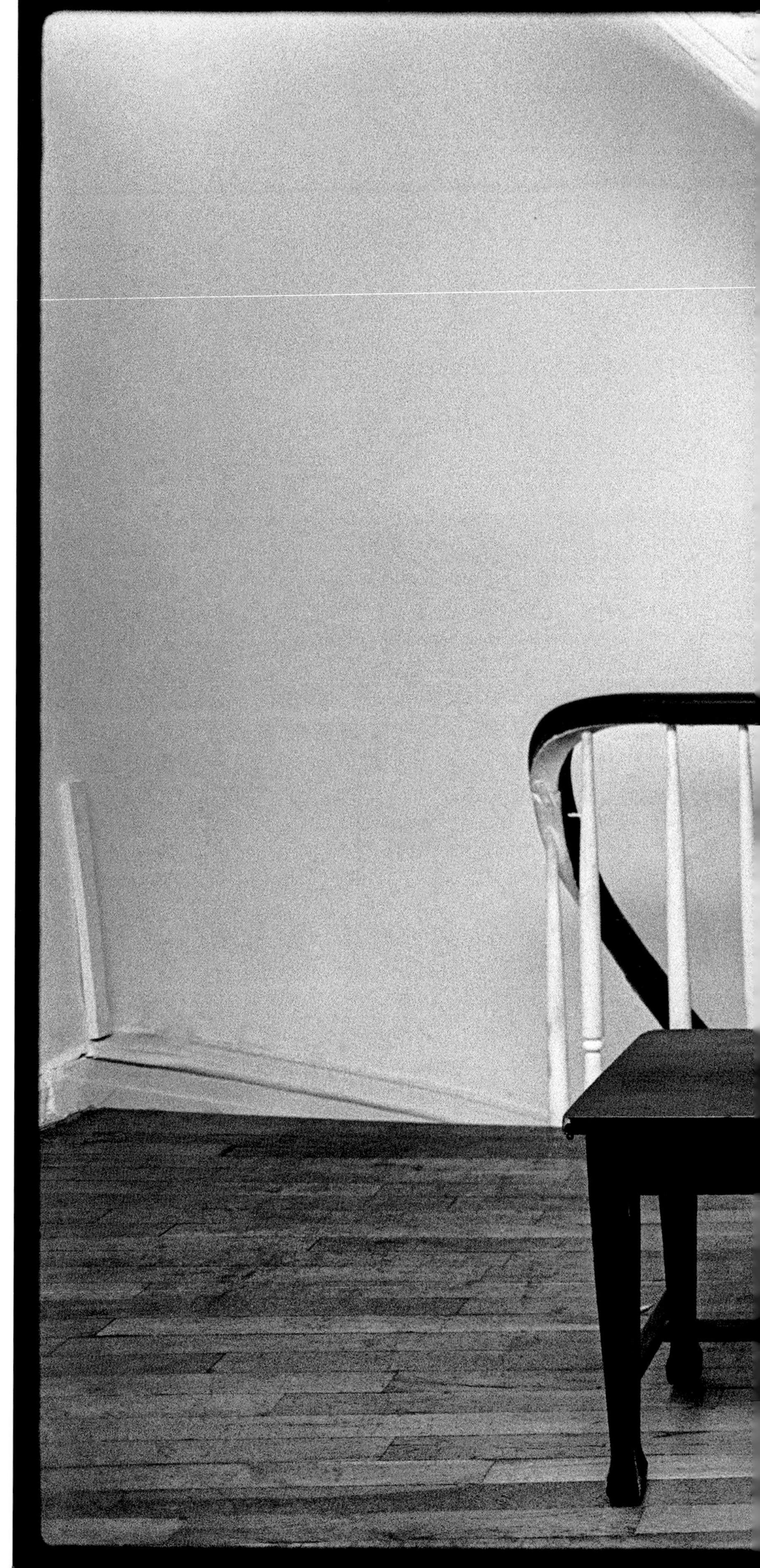

DR. JOHN, 1982

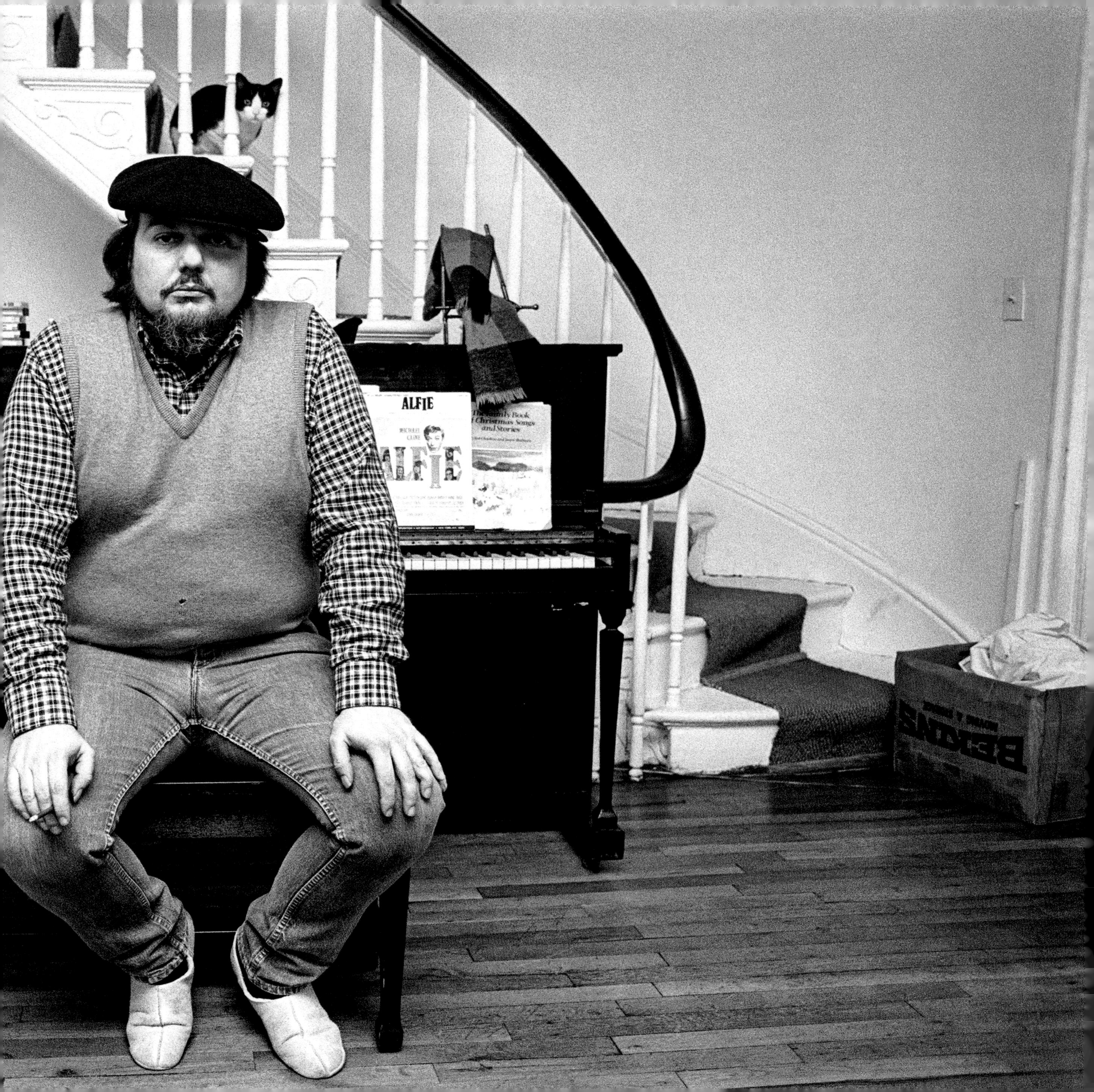

ALFIE
MICHAEL CAINE
ALFIE
The Family Book
of Christmas Songs
and Stories
BEKINS

KURTIS BLOW, 1980

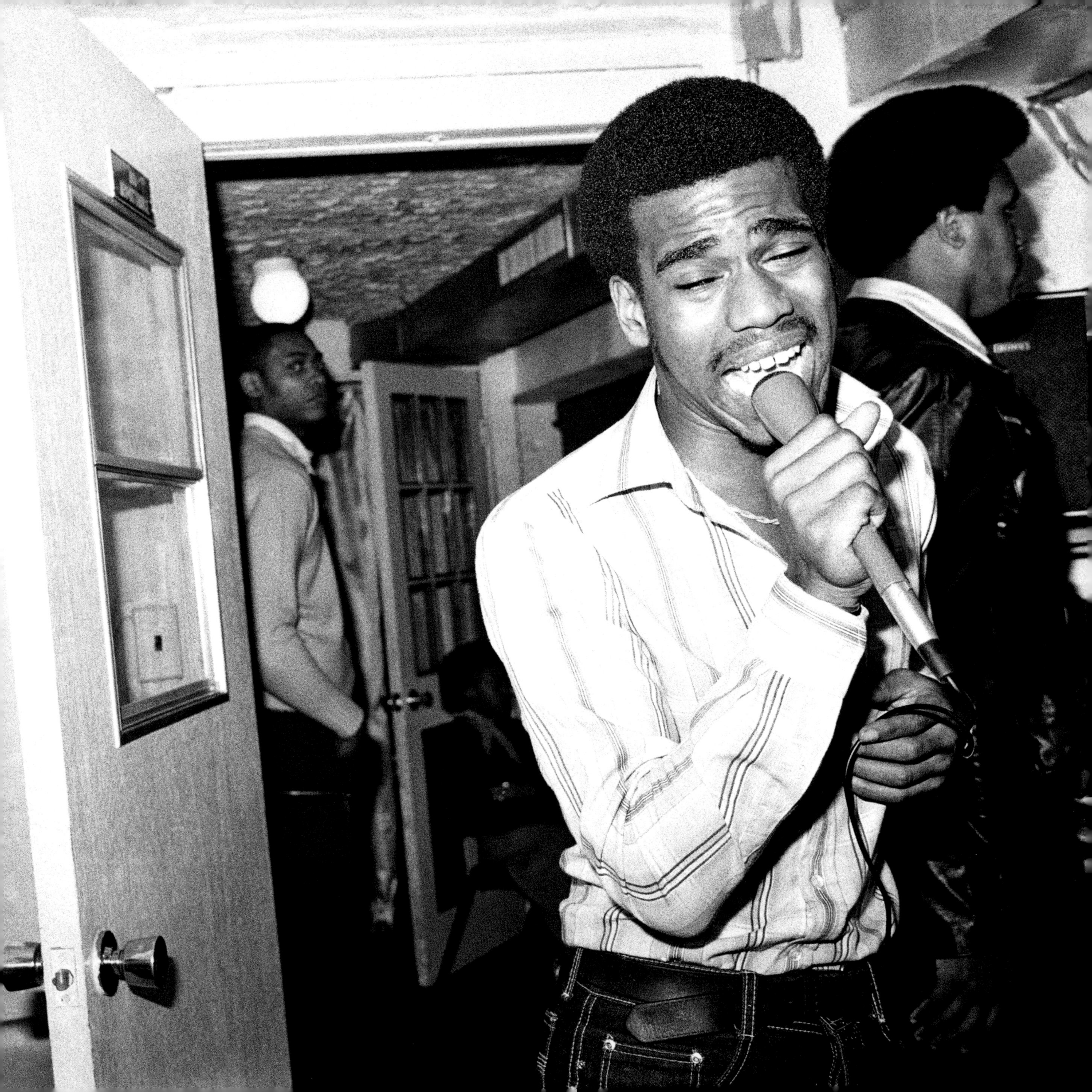

R.E.M., 1985

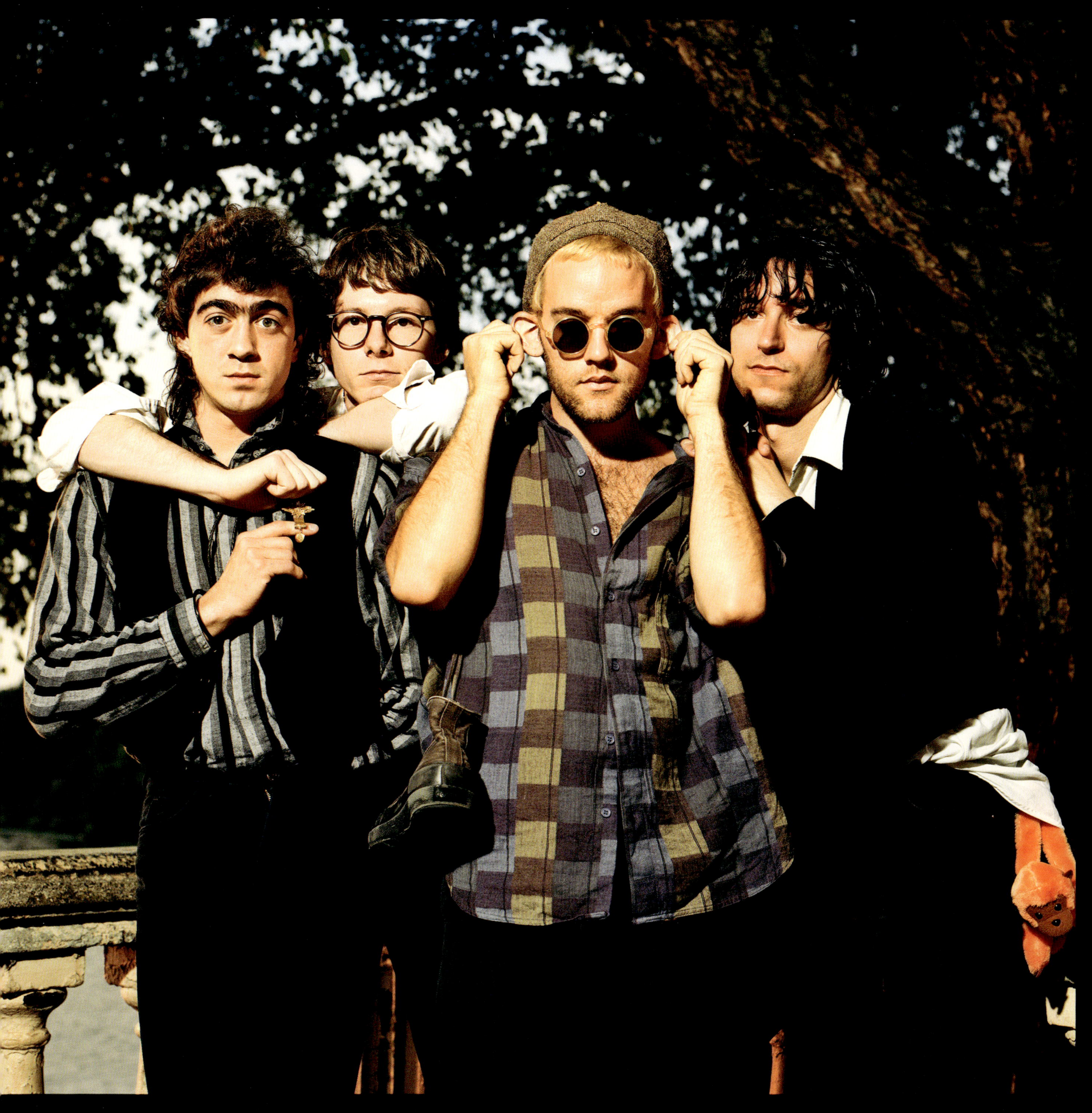

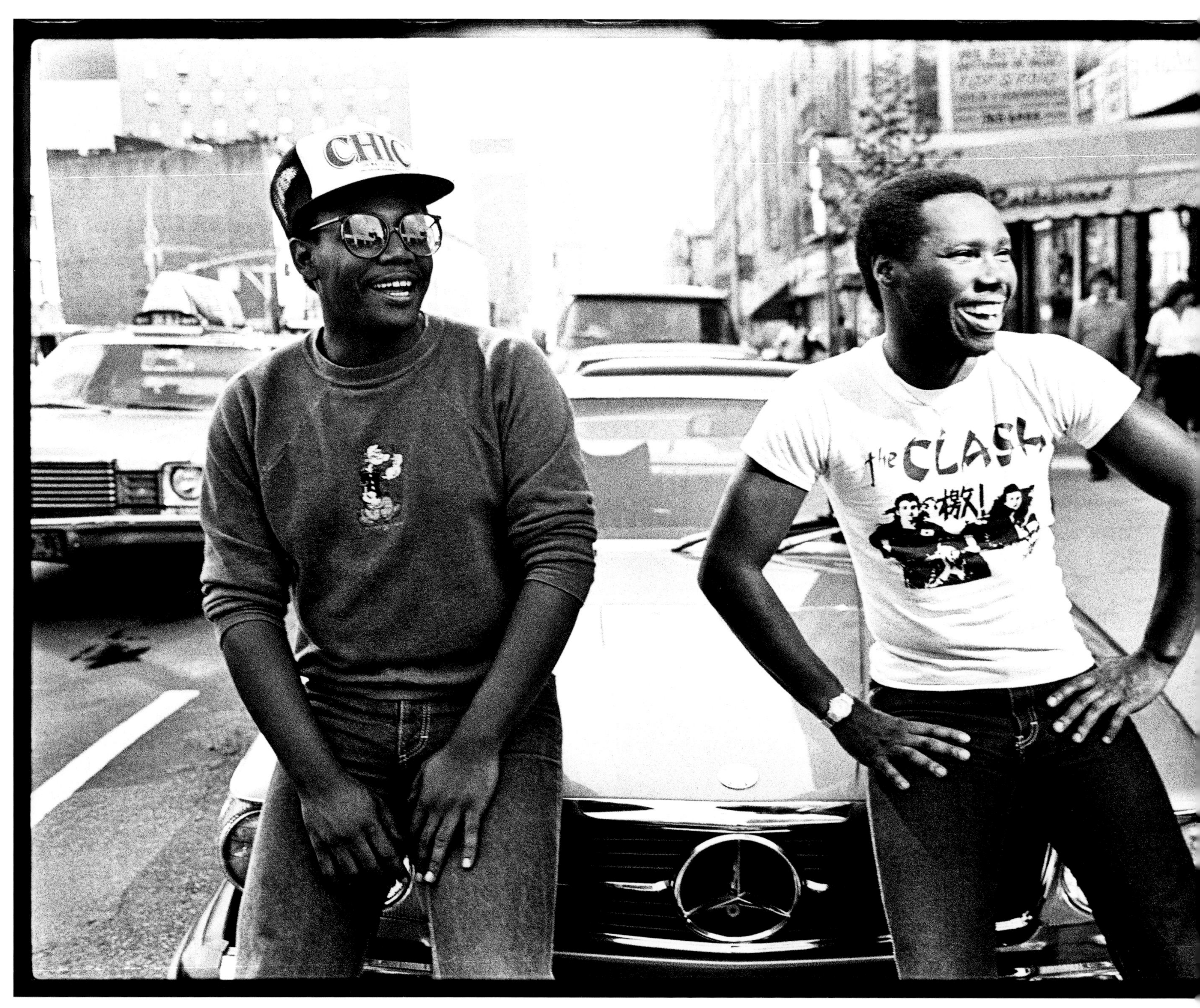

ABOVE: CHIC (BERNARD EDWARDS AND NILE RODGERS), 1980; OPPOSITE: ALICIA KEYS, 2002
PAGE 104: BEASTIE BOYS, 1987; PAGE 105: FRANK ZAPPA, 1988

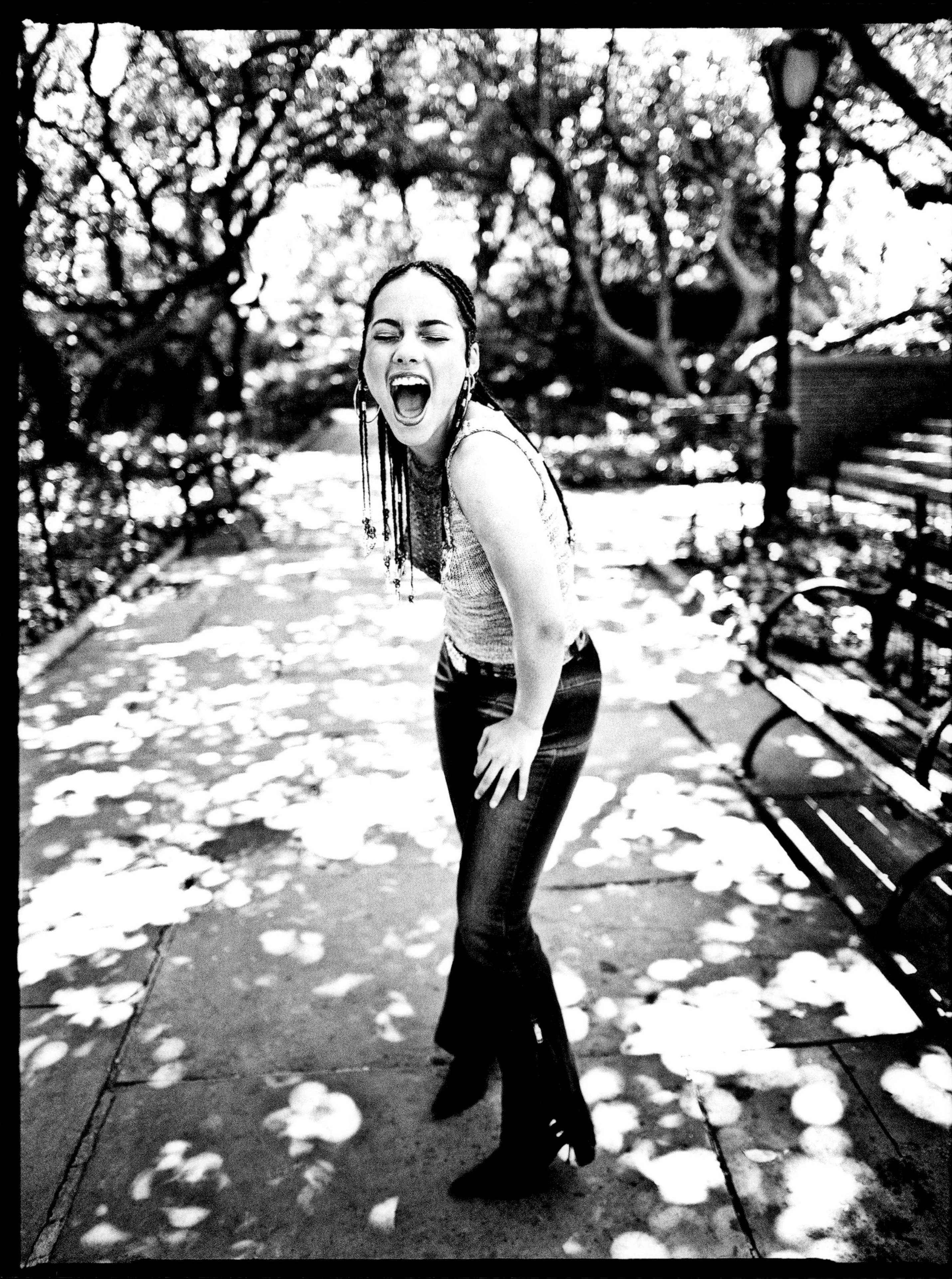

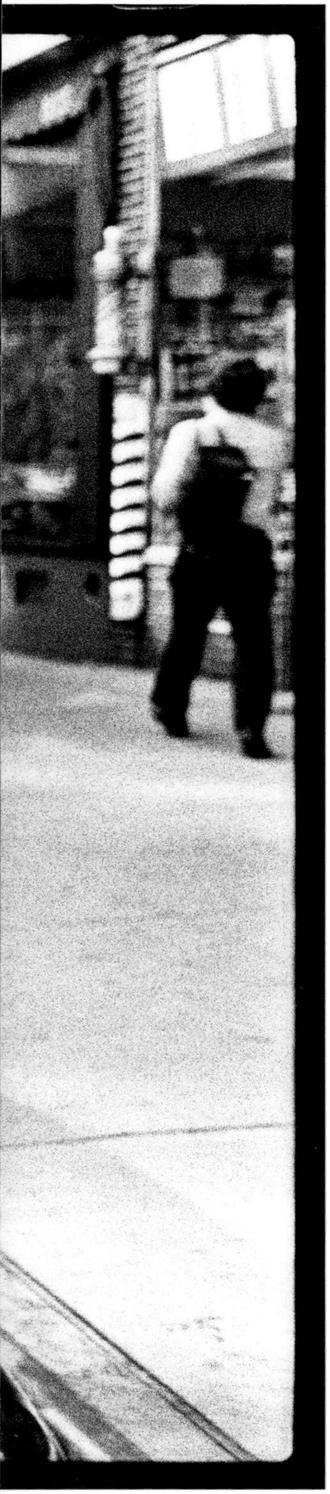

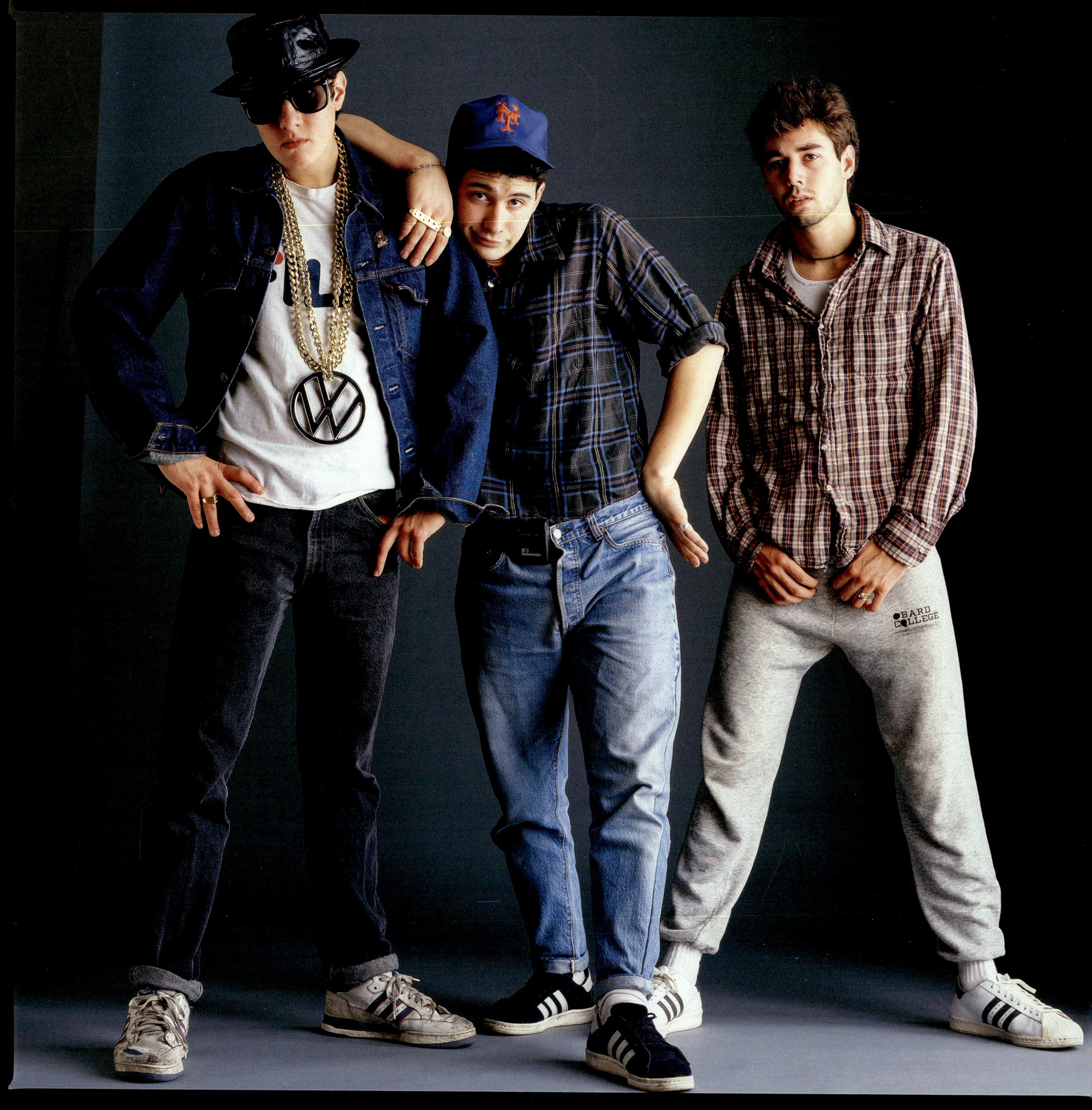

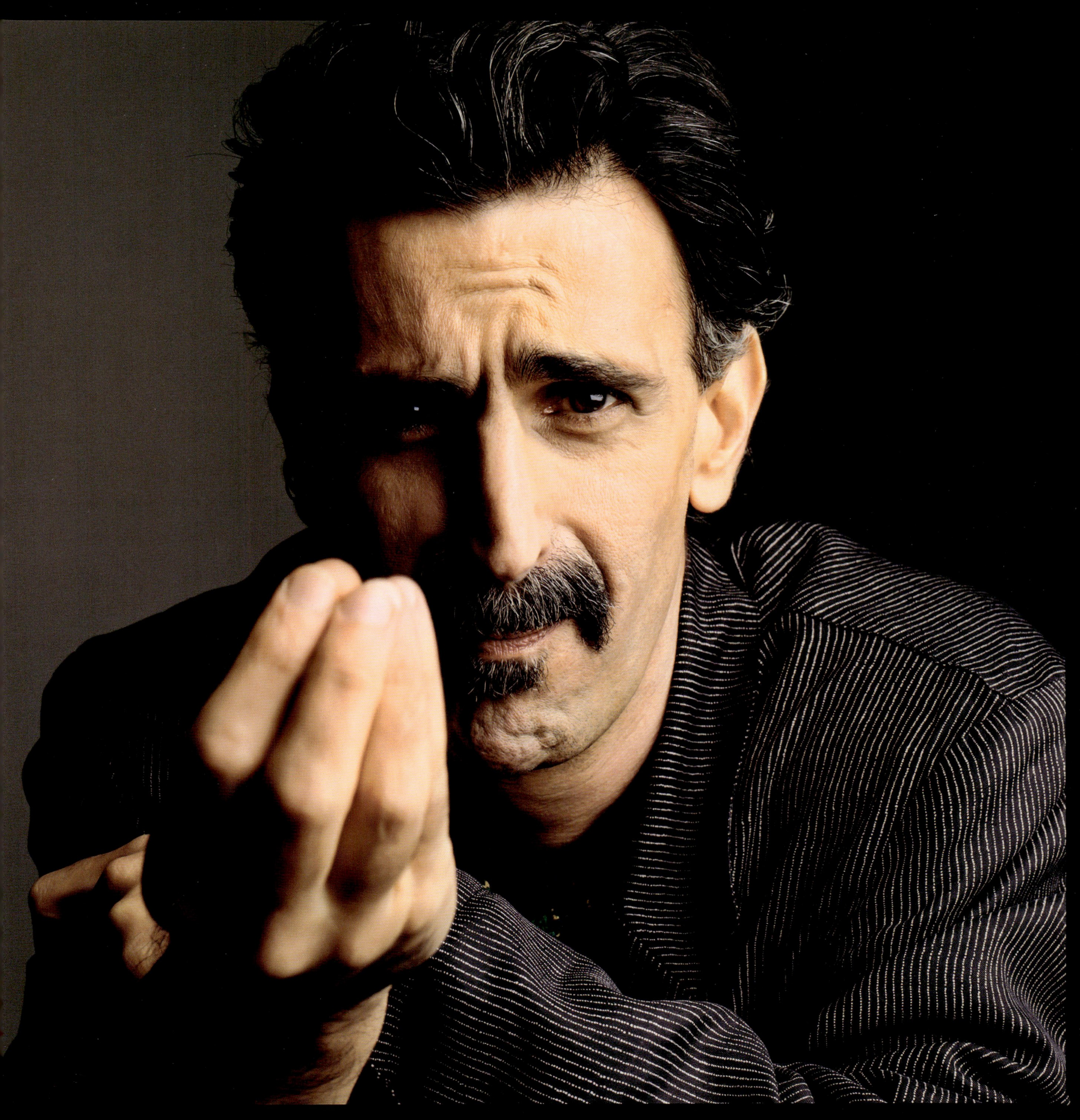

For my daughter, Molly Brown.

Acknowledgements:

Andrea Albertini, Edward Allan Baker, Rex Bonomelli, Bonnie Briant, Yolanda Cuomo,
Anthony DeCurtis, Elaine and Jerry Elovitz, Sam and Alyce Feingold, Chris Fladgate, John Fontana,
Sam Holdsworth, David Jackson, Mick Jagger, Lee Joseph, Sue Anne Johnson, Laurie Kratochvil,
Scott Lee, Diane Luger, Melanie Martinez, Will Maupin, Fred McDarrah, Matt McGinley, Karen Moline,
Michael Nagin, Miriam Parker, Michael Pietsch, Mario Pulice, Aaron Rapoport,
Donna Russo Schinderman, Stephen Shipps, Rene Varriano

My sincere thanks to all of the musicians.

Deborah Feingold
Music

Cover: Mick Jagger, 1987
Frontispiece: B.B. King, 1985

Book Design by Yolanda Cuomo Design, NYC
Associate Designer: Bonnie Briant

[DAMIANI]

Bologna, Italy
info@damianieditore.com
www.damianieditore.com

Printed in April 2014 by Grafiche Damiani, Italy.

ISBN 978-88-6208-311-9